TEACHERS MATTER

TEACHERS MATTER

Rethinking How Public Schools Identify, Reward, and Retain Great Educators

MARCUS A. WINTERS

ROWMAN & LITTLEFIELD PUBLISHERS, INC.

Lanham • Boulder • New York • Toronto • Plymouth, UK

Published by Rowman & Littlefield Publishers, Inc.
A wholly owned subsidiary of The Rowman & Littlefield Publishing Group, Inc.
4501 Forbes Boulevard, Suite 200, Lanham, Maryland 20706
http://www.rowmanlittlefield.com

Estover Road, Plymouth PL6 7PY, United Kingdom

British Library Cataloguing in Publication Information Available

Library of Congress Cataloging-in-Publication Data Available

ISBN 978-1-4422-1077-6 (cloth : alk. paper)
ISBN 978-1-4422-1079-0 (electronic)

∞™ The paper used in this publication meets the minimum requirements of
American National Standard for Information Sciences—Permanence of Paper
for Printed Library Materials, ANSI/NISO Z39.48-1992.

Printed in the United States of America

CONTENTS

FOREWORD

Joel Klein

Education reform is now a big issue generating lots of government activity, amidst lots of books, documentaries, television specials, and blog posts. As both a participant and observer in this now decade long discussion, I am most struck by how much the debate has changed in two interrelated ways recently.

First, there is much more support now than there was a decade ago for the view that "demography isn't destiny," meaning education can substantially improve children's opportunities in life, even for those who are raised in environments with the most challenges. Certainly poverty or a troubled family can make some children more difficult to educate, but now substantial evidence shows much better educational outcomes if that same child is properly schooled. Low-income African American students in Boston and New York are way ahead of the very same kind of student group in Detroit and Los Angeles. And the difference in performance between similar kinds of students at different schools can be staggering, as the charter school network KIPP (the Knowledge is Power Program) and others have shown. Only education can explain those differences.

The second big difference, which is directly related to the first, is that, unlike in the past, the focus of reform has come to rest on teachers as the key drivers of better outcomes. When I became New York City's schools chancellor almost a decade ago, the school improvement discussion was centered around curricula, class size, extended school days, better student supports, and the like. These are obviously important things. But today there is wide agreement that, first and foremost, "teachers matter," as the title of this book flatly states. Unfortunately, it took far too long to recognize this.

For the past forty years America has been making a big bet on education that isn't panning out. Since 1970, we have increased our spending in real dollars 2 ½ times, expanded the ranks of teachers by almost two-thirds (from 2 million to more than 3.2 million), substantially raised teachers' salaries, and grown pre-K and afterschool programs.

The result? On the well-respected national high school exam (the National Assessment of Educational Progress), students' performance is flat in reading and math, and has decreased slightly in science. This is a remarkable story of policy failure across the nation, through policies largely set by states moving essentially in lock step. Federalists beware!

In retrospect, the reason for this failure is obvious: a smaller class, longer day, or extra year won't measurably change outcomes unless our students have great teachers. Has anyone ever heard a student's parent express preference for a class of twenty led by a poor teacher over a class of thirty led by a great one?

In short, we made a misguided bet on quantity, with more teachers and more time spent in the classroom, rather than on quality—namely having better teachers. This strategy has suited the teachers' unions just fine. More teachers mean more members, more dues, and more power. But this strategy didn't work for the kids.

The recent shift has been seismic. While smaller classes and better across-the-board teacher pay are still part of the education discussion, I can't overemphasize how dramatically the conversation is now focused on teacher effectiveness. President Barack Obama put it this way: "The single most important factor in determining [student] achievement is not the color of their skin or where they come from. It's not who their parents are or how much money they have. It's who their teacher is." It would have been politically unimaginable for a previous Democratic candidate for president to say that.

But beneath this newly emerged consensus on the importance of teacher effectiveness lies a much deeper division: those who want to hire the kind of teachers we need, versus those who want to keep working around those we have. The reformers want: (1) much greater accountability for teachers, based on rigorous qualitative and quantitative evaluations; (2) a compensation system that rewards excellence monetarily without being overwhelmingly back-loaded; (3) the ability to remove poor-performing teachers; and (4) the end of dysfunctional policies such as "last-hired, first fired."

Additionally, the reformers also want to give families—especially low-income families—greater choice through charter and public school options. And some reformers support private-school vouchers as well.

But the teachers' unions and their political supporters—including a few vocal academics—continue to defend the current system built essentially on lock-step pay, lifetime tenure, seniority preferences in pay, hiring and firing, and outsized post-employment benefits. Moreover, this group opposes choice—especially when it includes non-unionized options such as charters or private schools—and insists on protecting a government-run monopoly that ensures that students—and, consequently, teacher jobs—are not lost to new competitors.

This dispute is both extremely important and highly polarized. For the last several years, the reformers clearly have been gaining ground. The media, through editorial and op-ed pages, have been generally supportive, and films such as *Waiting for Superman* and *The Lottery* have galvanized the issue. More importantly, several states—under both Democratic and Republican governors—have recently adopted legislation embodying core parts of the reformist agenda. Indeed, much of this change is driven by President Obama and Secretary Arne Duncan's signature education initiative, called Race to the Top, which provides large financial incentives for states to support greater teacher accountability and more student choice. In addition, states and large urban school districts, virtually without exception, are now appointing commissioners and superintendents with demonstrated reformist credentials. Cities such as New York, Washington, D.C., and New Orleans, in particular, have developed significant choice systems that have threatened the union-controlled, monopoly public system. This is all a big deal.

But make no mistake: we are still in the very early innings of real reform, and the well-resourced defenders of the status quo are digging in for a substantial and protracted game. At stake, in my view, is nothing less than the future of our country. We simply cannot continue on a path of educational failure in a globalized, twenty-first-century economy.

Marcus Winters jumps into this bubbling cauldron of political and policy debate feet first with this thoughtful new book about teacher effectiveness. Though much has already been said on this topic, two things about this book stand out immediately. First, Winters is a careful researcher, who believes that research should matter in driving policy a lot more than it does now– so this book is long on analysis and short on rhetoric. And second, though Winters has a long track record of arguing for the importance of increasing school choice, he believes we will continue to have a monolithic public education system for a long time, so we need to take seriously attempts to fix it. In his words, "There is not enough supply in the private or charter sector to compete seriously with public schools, nor will there be any time in the near future."

While it is true that private schools and charters enroll a relatively small portion of students nationally, I know Winters would agree that in specific situations, increased competition can put important pressure on the existing system to change. For example, that is precisely what happened in Washington, D.C. where charter schools took away large numbers of students from the traditional public school system, and ultimately helped Chancellor Michelle Rhee get her ground-breaking contract with the union. But Winters is surely right that, whatever the role of competition, reform of the existing public-school system is essential. As Willie Sutton said about the banks and money, that's where the kids are.

To that end, Winters sets for himself two important goals at the outset: "The first is to show that the way we hire, train, compensate, and evaluate public school teachers actually reduces teacher quality. The second, more difficult, goal is to sketch an alternative system that is capable of *improving* teacher quality." As if the challenge he set for himself is not difficult enough, Winters then has the audacity to argue that his proposals will "benefit the entire teaching profession." This will come as news to those, such as the unions, who have long fought against many of the policies that Winters proposes.

To make his case, Winters takes us through several critical policy arenas, starting first with teacher evaluation. As he correctly points out, although everyone appears to agree that some teachers are extraordinary, and others are, frankly, awful, there is little agreement on how to measure these differences. I personally believe that much of the opposition to a meaningful evaluation system comes from those who don't want to differentiate, and therefore don't want to evaluate. Consequently, whatever criteria are proposed, these critics find fault without proposing a meaningful alternative.

Wisely, for his part, Winters is careful not to over-sell any particular evaluation criterion—because none is perfect—but ends up asking exactly the right question: "Which is worse, a false positive (a teacher who is good but found bad under an evaluation system) or a false negative (a teacher who is bad but found good under the same evaluation system)?" The unions understandably fight to minimize false positives. But who fights to minimize false negatives—that is, those teachers who are failing children?

Winters then tackles existing practices, which he convincingly shows are hurting kids and undermining the teaching profession. None of the issues he addresses is uncontroversial, though Winters presents them so fairly and even-handedly that it is hard to see how anyone could disagree with his proposed solutions. He shows, for example, that teacher credentialing—undergraduate degrees, masters' degrees, and randomly selected extra coursework—is worthless when it comes to a teacher's effectiveness. So let's stop paying huge amounts of money for education schools and courses that don't add value. In Winters' words, let's "eliminate costly barriers to entry."

Next, Winters trains his sights on the twin reforms that the defenders of the current public-school system most resist: paying the good teachers more and getting rid of the bad ones. He shows that, currently, the best economic reason for going into teaching is that, regardless of performance, it is almost impossible to get fired. You get steady raises with seniority, which are then followed by exceptional post-employment lifetime pension and health benefits. In short, while teachers don't get rich, once they start teaching, typically in their early twenties, they are reasonably set for life.

Expanding on his concerns about post-employment benefits, Winters further demonstrates their unfortunate lock-in effects on employees. After a decade or so spent teaching, employees would be irrational to leave the system until their rights to these benefits fully vest. This incentivizes teachers to stick around, sometimes for decades, whether or not they are engaged or effective. A better idea, Winters argues, is to pay teachers like most people are paid: fairly during the time they actually work, while letting them decide how much to set aside for their retirement.

The soundness that Winters envisions is closer than ever before, but is still far off, at least in most places. The power of this book, however, should accelerate the pace of necessary change. There is much here to absorb, so read carefully and enjoy.

INTRODUCTION

Marie and Charles began teaching at the same inner-city public elementary school seven years ago, after completing their masters' degrees in education at the same prominent state university where they took most of their classes together. Now they are both fifth-grade teachers, handling approximately twenty-eight kids each year. But that's where the similarities end.

Everyone in the school privately agrees that Marie is by far the best teacher in the building. Her class of low-income, mostly minority students walk through her door barely literate, but by the end of the school year the boys and girls have advanced two grade levels—not one—in reading, on average.

In stark contrast, Charles's students leave his class with only half a grade increase in reading proficiency. They are on par with the majority of the other children in a school whose test scores consistently rank among the worst in the state. Charles believes that his students lag behind because their poverty imposes insurmountable challenges and their parents aren't dedicated enough to keep them on the right track.

Knowledgeable parents clearly prefer their children be enrolled in Marie's class. Why, then, does the public school system respond by treating these very different teachers as though they are identical?

Both Marie and Charles are evaluated as "satisfactory" each year by their school's officials. They earn identical salaries. Each received the job protection of tenure in the first year of eligibility, without any objections from school administrators. As far as the school system is concerned, Charles and Marie are interchangeable.

Marie and Charles are a hypothetical example. But their story represents a very real problem in American public schools today. There are many great teachers like Marie filling our classrooms. But there are many mediocre—and worse—teachers in American classrooms as well. Anyone who has experience with a public school as an employee, parent, or student knows those facts to be true.

But the current system for employing public school teachers makes no attempt to distinguish between the Charleses and Maries of the world either before or after they have entered the classroom.

This book explores the human consequences of an employment system that refuses to acknowledge the different levels of effectiveness of its teachers. By accumulating and interpreting the lessons provided by modern research about the role teachers play in our public schools, and by exploring the consequences of those findings, I intend to prove that those lessons are nothing less than devastating for public school students. The basic assumptions underlying how their teachers are trained, recruited, and compensated—assumptions that may appear quite reasonable to the casual observer—have turned out to be inconsistent with the proven facts.

THE FLAWED STRUCTURE OF THE CURRENT SYSTEM

The current system scrutinizes only the tangibles that a teacher brings into the classroom, but makes little effort to examine the outcomes of his teaching, in the form of student learning. It pays a great deal of attention to easily observable characteristics about teachers—such as their years of experience and the number of advanced degrees they hold—and then essentially assumes they are performing well in the classroom. If a teacher has ticked all the right boxes before he begins work in the current system, how well his students learn is of little consequence to his teaching career.

Over time, a teacher will earn a salary that is below that of the average white-collar professional with a college degree. However, she will also work fewer hours, enjoy much stronger job security, and receive far better health and pension benefits than the average professional. She may choose to work long, difficult hours preparing her lessons and tutoring her students, but her decision to do so will have no bearing on her salary, advancement, or pension.

The primary assumption made by the current public school system is that a teacher's effectiveness in the classroom can be accurately explained by her training and experience. *And that basic assumption has turned out to be false.* There is *no* evidence that earning more credentials influences a teacher's effectiveness, and any benefits accrued by teaching experience plateau after only a few years in the classroom.

Clearly, this research points us to a system for employing public school teachers that is very different from the one we use today.

A PRO-TEACHER DISCUSSION

Americans hold few collective treasures dearer than their public schools. Most living American adults attended a public school in their youth. The vast majority of parents of school-aged children send their sons and daughters to their neighborhood public school. The success of universal public education is perhaps the most important reason for the hegemony achieved by the United States during the twentieth century.[1]

Teachers are the face of the great American public school system. For many, public school teachers represent the promise that education holds for a child's life and the nation's future. Most of us who have achieved success can point to at least one teacher who inspired us. Great teachers can provide students with the tools they need to overcome life's most difficult obstacles. Because we hold a special place in our heart for public school teachers, it is difficult to offer criticism of the job some of them do.

Some policy makers are hesitant to consider changes to the current teaching system because many teachers (and their union representatives) so vocally support the status quo. Those who support the current system frequently argue that reforms meant to address teacher quality make teachers "scapegoats" for low student performance.[2] Teachers, we are told, feel under attack. According to these critics, she who supports reform disrespects teachers and fails to recognize their importance in the classroom.

Ironically, true reform means focusing more on classroom performance, not less.

If we are serious when we assert that teachers are our schools' most essential asset, we cannot continue to treat all teachers as if they perform the same. We do not honor effective teaching when we ignore the undeniable fact that teachers are not equally effective in the classroom. There is no meaningful difference between treating teachers as if they are identical and treating them as if they don't matter.

The reforms proposed in this book would offer effective teachers far more reward than they earn in the current system. Effective teachers deserve to be recognized by an evaluation system that takes seriously the contribution they are making to their students' lives. We should reward effective teachers with higher salaries. Conversely, weeding out poor teachers will benefit not just children, but the entire teaching profession.

Reforming the employment system for public school teachers is a pro-teacher agenda. The many great teachers in America's public schools today are excelling *despite* the structure of the system that employs them, not because of it. That's not the way it should be. A system that respects the difficulty of the job and the important contributions that teachers make to society is one that acts on the truth that some teachers are excellent, and some people simply don't belong in the classroom—even if they did manage to graduate from a teaching college.

THREE GUIDING PRINCIPLES

This book proposes three basic principles that will illuminate the shortfalls of the current system, as well as highlight what needs improvement. If these three basic ideas are judged as sound, then it will necessarily follow that the current system does our schools a disservice.

Principle 1—The Most Important Goal of Public Schools is Educating Students

Public schools are many things to many people. They are one of the few places in the modern world that bring an entire community together in a shared physical setting. Public school systems employ millions of people, and not all of them are teachers. When one factors in school administrators, support staff, custodians, bus drivers, cafeteria workers, and so on, it's easy to understand how in many cases the public school system is the largest employer in the community. Public schools have been vehicles for social integration, and they are an important conduit of knowledge and values between the established community and the next generation.

Public schools justifiably serve a variety of society's purposes. But first and foremost, they are places where students are meant to learn. The primary responsibility of public schools is to ensure that students gain proficiency in the skills and subjects necessary to obtain personal and professional success. Public schools cannot be considered successful if large groups of students leave school without the basic skills necessary to succeed in the modern world.

It might seem uncontroversial to suggest that the success of public schools depends primarily on whether students are learning. Everyone pays lip service to that basic premise. But unfortunately, not everyone acts as if the goal of public schools ought to be student learning. The goals of those who work within schools are not always aligned with those of students. And that is the most important policy problem facing those who would reform the education system.

If policies benefited both students and teachers equally, there would be little argument about how to structure public schools. Unfortunately, we will see there are many cases in which the interests of students and their teachers do not align (for example, when poorly performing or abusive teachers are protected by the rules intended to outlaw arbitrary firing). The interests of employees and employers are never perfectly aligned. Thus, we shouldn't be surprised that there are times when teachers benefit from policies that do not benefit their students. The reforms I propose would realign schools primarily toward the interests of the students, while also benefiting teachers. Teachers are, after all, employees working within a large bureaucratic system that ought to value student achievement above everything else.

Principle 2—Public Schools Are Not Profit-Making Firms

Much has been made of the virtue of trying to run schools "like a business." But public schools are not corporations. Public schools do not operate in a commercial marketplace; they are a public service similar to police and fire departments. This reality has substantial consequences for what we might expect from education reform, but it is often lost in both the academic and popular discussion of many public education reform strategies.

One position often expressed by teachers' unions—and others—is that public schools are so removed from the private sector that incentive structures simply won't work. According to this view, public schools are a special case. Those who work in public schools operate at maximum capacity at all times on their own accord and thus do not respond to external motivations in the way that workers in the private sector do. But this idea is countered by a great deal of research indicating that students, schools, teachers, and entire education systems do in fact change their behavior when policy makers alter their incentive structures. A wide body of research suggests that public schools improve in response to accountability policies[3] as well as to competition from school choice programs.[4]

However, it is equally dangerous to assume, as do many economists and education reform advocates, that public schools operate no differently from private firms. Public schools are funded and operated by the government and are thus insulated from many important market mechanisms to which private firms are forced to respond. When considering changes that relate to things such as teacher quality, it is important to keep in mind the differences between market forces and other types of incentives.

Many believe that American education would benefit from operating in a market environment. However, for better or worse, we do not live in that world. Recent advances in school voucher policies and charter schools have increased the competition that faces public schools, and research suggests that such competition has led to improved performance of some public schools.[5] However, significantly less than 1 percent of students use a voucher to pay private school tuition, and only 3 percent of students currently attend charter schools. There is not enough supply in the private or charter sector to compete seriously with public schools, nor will there be any time in the near future.

In addition, we must keep in mind that teachers are not identical to private sector workers. Teachers are college graduates who have chosen to enter a field with relatively low salaries. Most teachers enter the profession at least in part because they like working with children and have a true desire to see them succeed. These realities cannot be ignored when considering reforms to the system that employs public school teachers. Of course, teachers are people, and people respond to incentives. However, we should recognize that our schools are staffed largely with individuals motivated by altruism as well as by material reward, and that has important consequences for what we might expect from certain reforms.

Of course, we can look to examples from the private sector when considering how to improve the public school system. But we must use discretion and careful consideration of how such changes will operate within the structure of the public school system. If we operated schools as if they were subject to market principles, we would be sorely disappointed in the result. The foundational and operational differences between private firms and schools are more in degree than in kind, but they are real and are important enough that we must take them seriously.

Principle 3—Empirical Research Can Play an Important Role in Crafting Education Policy

We rely on empirical research to inform public policy in multiple arenas. Communities commission researchers to evaluate the likely economic effects for developing new ventures. The FDA depends on tests of a drug's effects before allowing it to go to market. Lawmakers look to advice from economists and others when considering tax cuts or spending proposals, and so on.

However, the idea that we can improve public schools through empirical research is relatively new. Until very recently, research in the field of education has lagged behind that of other social sciences. Qualitative research dominated the discussion, while the relegation of empirical research to the back burner had to do both with the culture surrounding schools and the fact that researchers lacked the data necessary to conduct meaningful empirical evaluations. Both of those situations have changed in the past decade.

Some are hesitant to take seriously empirical research on public schools. Skeptics argue, with some merit, that public schools are complex organizations that cannot be reduced to a single or a few numbers.

Certainly, quantitative analysis cannot tell us everything we want to know about schools. But it has several attractive features. For instance, empirical research helps us to identify trends that escape mere observation, and an overall perspective that can overcome the biases of educators and researchers working within a school. When conducted honestly, empirical research does not depend on a particular researcher, but rather creates tests that can be replicated across schools. Furthermore, empirical researchers have access to the same data sets and can thus check each other to ensure that analyses are properly conducted. The notion that there are "lies, damn lies, and statistics" has far more to do with improper interpretation of empirical findings than with how they are calculated.

PLAN FOR THIS BOOK

Writing a book about teacher quality is sure to ruffle a few feathers. Many are uncomfortable even raising the idea that perhaps at least part of the problem in education has to do with teachers. Teachers don't like being questioned about their ability to do their jobs any more than anyone else does. For a variety of reasons—not the least of which is that they entrust their children to their care every day—parents, policy makers, and journalists are inclined to give teachers the benefit of the doubt. Furthermore, many of us have direct experience with great teachers who have had a positive impact on our lives, leading us to conclude that teacher failure is more likely due to a lack of resources rather than lack of skill or desire. These human elements mean that discussing teacher quality is an emotional exercise, even compared to other hot-button issues like class size or curriculum.

But the public school system and America's students suffer greatly from our inability to engage in a rational discussion about teacher quality. Our squeamishness has created an environment where the debate is increasingly counterproductive and nonsensical. This book has two important goals. The first is to show that the way we hire, train, compensate, and evaluate public school teachers actually reduces teacher quality.

The second, more difficult, goal is to sketch an alternative system that is capable of *improving* teacher quality. I will lay out the basic argument for a new employment system that could more effectively recruit, retain, and motivate public school teachers. When we step back and take a broader perspective, there are some clear problems with the current system—and some clear solutions.

As in any industry, the employment system for public school teachers has important implications for nearly every aspect of the labor market: the type of person who decides to become a teacher, the type who decides to stay in the classroom, the extent to which those teachers are motivated to do their best work, and even the way that teacher quality is distributed across schools. The reforms discussed in this book are not mutually exclusive. Adopted individually, each would improve upon the current system. Adopted in concert, they have the opportunity to transform teaching and learning in the United States.

1

HOW DATA CAN HELP IMPROVE
PUBLIC SCHOOLS

We have recently learned a great deal about the role of teachers, their contribution to student learning, and the factors related to their success or failure. This increase in actionable information comes from a revolution in the use of empirical research to measure and understand public schools.

In his 2003 book *Moneyball*, Michael Lewis explained how in recent years the Oakland A's managed to post one of the highest winning percentages of any team in Major League Baseball despite consistently having one of its smallest payrolls.[1] The A's trick, it turns out, was a data-driven assessment for identifying players who would contribute to a team's success. Instead of relying on the traditional subjective analysis of baseball lifers and the usual array of official statistics, the team's general manager, Billy Beane, hired a group of numbers geeks to develop statistical models that could better predict a player's ability to produce runs in the future. Beane's insight, which was already percolating among baseball outsiders, was that a team with better information about player quality has an advantage on the field. Data analysis didn't ensure you'd win the World Series, but, all else being equal, it gave you a better opportunity to do so.

In hindsight, it's surprising that the smart people working in baseball before Beane came along thought that scouting reports correctly identified the best players. Scouts' evaluations were often based on little more than viewing a few of a player's at bats. Nonetheless, for little more reason than clinging to tradition, clubs simply did not bother to improve upon these clearly incomplete measures of a player's worth for many decades. Failure to distinguish correctly between the most and least effective players cost teams tens of millions of dollars each year as they overpaid for mediocre talent.

As in baseball, many features of the current system for employing public school teachers seem reasonable on the surface. For example, it seems self-evident that experienced teachers and teachers who have earned advanced degrees would be more effective than their junior colleagues.

Sports franchises have recognized that they can use data to identify inefficiencies that will save them money and increase their performance. Policy makers have used advances in the development and use of data to save lives.

In the early 1990s, New York City was a pretty difficult place to live. Crime was out of control, and it appeared that there was little that could be done about it.[2]

Then came CompStat. Adopted by Mayor Rudolph Giuliani under the guidance of his police chief, William Bratton, this revolutionary data system tracked crime precisely. The influx of data allowed the NYPD to focus its efforts on the most troubled neighborhoods, and to hold precinct captains accountable when things went wrong.

Looking back, you have to wonder why it took so long for the police to adopt CompStat. Identifying the areas where crime is persistent would seem essential to anticipating it. Once technology was capable of maintaining and analyzing information about street crime, the obvious next step was to put such data to good use. Public schools are only now beginning to learn the fundamental lessons of *Moneyball* and CompStat.

The policies governing teachers and schools were not developed without consideration of their effects on student achievement, though student achievement was not the only variable in the consideration. However, it has become clear over time that what works for teachers does not necessarily work for students.

The bread-and-butter issues in education policy beg for objective, quantifiable answers. How many teachers are great, how many are adequate, and how many are underperforming? What difference will your child's specific teacher make in your child's experience? How much does a teacher benefit from earning an advanced degree or gaining another five years of experience? How much does it matter if a teacher was trained in an alternative certification program rather than a conventional program at a college of education? What characteristics are related to a teacher's effectiveness in the classroom? The list of questions that could benefit from objective answers goes on and on.

There are limits to how well subjective observation can answer questions like the above. Our eyes are not able to see everything that makes one teacher more effective than others. Objective analyses with quantifiable results are far better at producing answers to those questions—and many others.

We are in the midst of an empirical revolution in education policy. The new widespread availability of quantitative data measuring student performance has allowed us to answer a variety of questions that we couldn't begin to answer before. The role quantitative analysis plays in explaining our world has increased at a rapid pace in the past several decades. The power of modern computers increases our ability to store and analyze information, and several fields in the social sciences have moved in the direction of quantitative analysis in order to better describe our world. Though there is already an established history of quantitative research in many fields, its use in understanding relationships within schools is not yet twenty years old.

This influx of empirical research in education policy provides us with truly game-changing information about the effectiveness of the policies that govern the current public school system. It turns out that our eyes have been lying to us: many assumptions that we have taken for granted about our public schools and public school teachers have been false. We will return to this point shortly.

EDUCATION AS A SOCIAL SCIENCE

Education researchers were actually at the forefront of the push toward empirical, scientifically based research in the twentieth century. Some of the earliest social science experiments utilizing modern, random-assignment research techniques were evaluations of public school effectiveness. But the discipline began to minimize these approaches at precisely the same time that professionals in other social sciences began to prioritize quantitative analysis.[3] Education research became dominated by those who believed that schools were too complex and heterogeneous for empirical evaluations of entire systems to hold meaning. Rather than follow the scientific revolutions going on within other disciplines, researchers in education followed what sociologist Thomas Cook called an R&D model based on various forms of management consulting.[4]

We can learn a great deal from qualitative research. However, what Cook referred to as the "sciencephobia" in education research during the 1980s and 1990s left a major void in our understanding of the effectiveness of policies operating within public schools.[5] The most important questions in education policy research are questions of cause and effect. Do school-choice policies influence student achievement? Are some teachers more effective than others? Does a teacher's performance improve over time and with additional training? Empirical research across large school systems, particularly for those that use or replicate experimental techniques, is far better at answering such big questions.

What produced the shift toward prioritizing empirical research in education? The most-often cited, and likely the dominant reason, is the expansion of data on student academic performance. When schools began to test systematically large groups of students, they created a treasure trove of quantitative data about student proficiency—output of education—that had previously been lacking. Economists and other quantitative researchers took notice once there was something of interest that could be measured.

Though its wide use is a relatively new phenomenon, standardized testing itself has a long history in the United States. New York State's Regent's examinations have been administered since the mid-nineteenth century. Testing has been widespread in the United States since at least the 1950s, when school systems began administering tests such as the Iowa Test of Basic Skills primarily to gauge student performance and drive pedagogical instruction. Standardized testing expanded throughout the twentieth century, and took new significance in 1983 when the blockbuster report by the National Commission on Excellence in Education titled "A Nation at Risk" pointed to the disappointing student performance on standardized tests as proof that America's schools had lost their way.[6]

"A Nation at Risk" spawned the modern standards and accountability-based reform movement that provides much of the framework for education policy today. In essence, this framework says that school systems need to have standards for the level of student proficiency, and it uses frequent standardized testing to measure the attainment of goals. The shift toward the standards-based approach produced a dramatic increase in standardized testing. Most states had already adopted and attached stakes to the results of standardized exams before the federal No Child Left Behind law in 2002 made testing third- through eighth-grade students in math and reading a universal requirement.

One factor driving the testing movement was the development of sophisticated systems to store all of this data. Since test scores were now used not only for diagnostic purposes but also to hold schools and students accountable for their achievement, the test scores needed to be collected and maintained. The most sophisticated data systems—found in Florida, Texas, North Carolina, Tennessee, Chicago, New York City, and some other school systems—linked individual student test scores to demographic information and sometimes also to information about the child's school and teachers.

These administrative data systems have proven to be a gold mine for quantitative researchers. Once a black box, suddenly there existed detailed, though imperfect, information on educational outputs—student proficiency—that could be used to measure and understand the relationship between public policies and school inputs on student academic achievement. The availability of these new and rich data sets piqued the interest of quantitative researchers, in particular economists, who pride themselves as the most quantitatively savvy of the social scientists.

The newfound interest in empirical research cannot be separated from the now overwhelming influence of economists in discussions of education policy. The expansion of the economics of education as a field has dramatically changed the way that researchers and policy makers think about public schools. This shift has consequences for nearly every part of education policy, not the least of which is the study of teacher quality.

Economists have been interested in education since the mid-twentieth century. Early work by Gary Becker, Jacob Mincer, and T. W. Schultz focused on the relationship between an individual's skills (that is, the quality of human capital) and earnings in the labor market. In a world where perfect data is nearly always absent, educational attainment was the best available measure of an individual's skills. The result was an important strand of research linking the quantity (and thus, it is supposed, the quality) of a person's education on his earnings.[7]

However, there was a bright line between the economists' work and research on the factors that make up effective schooling, which was more the province of sociologists and professors in education colleges. Economists were interested in the bigger picture—how did the results of education affect the economy generally?—than they were with the process that produced educational success. Those economists interested in the inner workings of schools and school systems (the field now known as the economics of education) were considered to be in a small subfield of labor economics.

When they engaged the education discussion, economists brought with them powerful statistical tools that vastly improved the quantitative methods previously used. New emphasis has been placed on using powerful social science techniques that mimic those used by the hard sciences.

Economists also bring their view of the world into the discussion of education policy. Most researchers in education colleges view education as an intimate procedure that differs dramatically across students and schools. Thus in the past, the study of education focused on a somewhat holistic understanding of the special circumstances of each school as its own organization. Economists, on the other hand, view the development of education as similar to any other production process. Organizations mix inputs (curriculum, class size, teacher quality, etc.) in order to produce an output (student proficiency).

Today, economists are at the cutting edge, evaluating and developing the framework for public education policies. Economists now serve with distinction in positions within the US Department of Education and are frequently hired to faculty positions in the policy departments of prestigious education colleges. The growing influence of the economic viewpoint in education is perhaps best illustrated by the movement toward standards-based accountability reforms that enforce performance goals for each school and school system.

Economists and other empirical researchers have used the new availability of rich data sets to study a variety of education policy issues. We now have information about student proficiency that is systematically collected, objective, and generally reliable. The influx of such data allows us to test and quantify relationships in education that were only suspected before.

One of the most important contributions made by empirical researchers in the past several years is the modeling and measurement of the effect that teachers have on student academic outcomes. This is still a growing and fruitful area of research, and one that has produced actionable information for policy makers. Because of this research, our understanding of the importance and makeup of teacher quality has grown substantially in only the last decade.

THE PROMISE AND LIMITS OF STANDARDIZED TESTS

Empirical researchers use statistical models to estimate the relationship between a child's teacher and her academic growth during the school year. Such models require a quantifiable and consistent measure of student learning. Standardized test scores are an obvious and useful tool for that purpose.

Standardized tests are very limited tools for measuring student proficiency. Even the best standardized tests can cover only a small number of skills. Students differ in their ability to handle the pressure and structure of the exam. Some students are better at test-taking skills—for instance, logically eliminating incorrect answers—that are not integral to the math and reading proficiency that the test is attempting to measure. Randomness plays a role in a student's performance through the types of questions that are asked, as well as the effects of a student's success at guessing answers.

Furthermore, tests measure only one or a few schooling outputs that are interesting to policy makers and parents. A truly effective teacher contributes to the lives of her students in several ways, not all of which are reflected in standardized math and reading exams. Ideally, we want to produce students who are not only literate and numerate but also who have a broader range of skills and knowledge.

Yet standardized test scores—particularly in math and reading—also have several attractive features for measuring student learning. First, scores on a well-constructed standardized exam provide an objective and reasonably accurate measure of the essential skills in which policy makers and the public are interested. We ask a lot from teachers, but their most important and basic task is to ensure that all students have the literacy and numeracy necessary to succeed in the modern world.

Standardized test scores are also the only tangible measures available to us that are objectively collected and have a uniform meaning across classrooms and schools. End-of-course grades are subjectively determined by teachers according to their own protocols. Principals may be able to accurately assess their own teachers—a proposition we will discuss more in the next chapter—but they may define effectiveness differently than a principal in another school and have no direct experience with teachers throughout the district or state.

Furthermore, thanks to the two-decades-old movement to increase standards and accountability, standardized test scores in reading and math are now ubiquitous. Most states had administered some sort of standardized exam to their students even before No Child Left Behind required them to do so. Today, every state tests each of its students in math and reading from grades three through eight.

Of course, even perfect measures of math and reading proficiency wouldn't tell us everything we want to know about a child's progress in school. We want teachers to inspire their students to be creative, purposeful, brave, tolerant, inquisitive, and active in the modern world. Nonetheless, numeracy and literacy are reasonable proxies and likely preconditions for the broader learning in which many are interested. If students are not becoming better readers in a particular third-grade teacher's classroom, they probably aren't gaining many other meaningful skills either. Reading and math are the building blocks on which so-called higher-order skills are developed.

Sadly, another reason to emphasize student math and reading when evaluating teacher quality is that far too many American students lack proficiency in these bedrock skills. We might be less interested in math and reading scores if the majority of students were excelling in these areas. For instance, schools where (just about) all students walk in the door as effective readers primarily derive their success from teaching students how to decipher and interpret increasingly more difficult material and to think critically about the world around them. Unfortunately, a disheartening number of America's kids lack the ability to understand even the most basic texts.

Fully one-third of American public school fourth-graders scored below the Basic level in reading on the National Assessment of Educational Progress (a highly respected standardized exam administered every other year to nationally representative samples of students by the US Department of Education.) More than half of African American and Hispanic students read below the Basic level. Nor are there a large numbers of American students with reading achievement high enough that it couldn't stand to be improved: only 7 percent of public school students scored at or above the Advanced level on the NAEP exam.[8] The modal achievement level for American fourth-graders is between the Basic and Proficient distinctions. That so many of America's students lack even basic literacy skills and so few of them have very high levels of reading proficiency requires that we focus on the attainment of these basic skills as a public policy matter.

Prioritizing test scores when we consider teacher quality and using standardized test scores to measure student progress does not mean that a high-quality teacher is one whose students end the year with highest test scores. Students arrive at school with advantages and disadvantages outside of a teacher's control, and that generally are reflected in their test scores. Students from wealthier families are more likely to have been read to by their parents when they were very young than students from more-disadvantaged backgrounds. Children with parents who went to college and hold professional jobs might have a clearer understanding of the importance and techniques required to obtain academic success.

If you want to find a teacher whose students have high test scores, you can greatly improve your odds by looking in schools that serve a predominantly white, relatively high-income student body. But that doesn't mean that all of the teachers in that school are effective. Nor is it necessarily the case that an urban school whose mostly poor and minority student body has very low test scores has ineffective teachers.

We ask public school teachers to make a difference with the students who walk through the door, regardless of their background. If her students are high achieving before they walk into a classroom, an effective teacher will push them to an even higher level. If her students start the year hardly able to read or do basic math problems, a good teacher will put them on the path toward literacy and numeracy. It is not within a public school teacher's power to eliminate the burdens of poverty. But all students can learn, and they will learn if they are assigned an effective teacher.

Students in a good teacher's classroom will have learned more at the end of a school year than they would have with a lower-quality teacher.

No matter how hard he tries, how much his students love him, what courses he has taken, what certificates he has earned, or how long he has been employed in the classroom, a teacher cannot be considered high-quality unless his students show academic progress commensurate with the abilities they bring into the classroom.

It's quite true that the inherent limits of standardized tests and the methods used to evaluate a teacher's influence on them are strong enough that we should not use them in isolation to evaluate a teacher's effectiveness. No responsible policy maker or researcher believes that tests should be used this way. Nonetheless, test scores are capable of broadly illustrating the relative effectiveness of public school teachers as a group and of raising red flags when a teacher is dramatically over- or underperforming relative to her peers. If students' test-score gains depend largely on the teacher who is in front of them, we can say with confidence that teacher quality is an important determinant of student learning.

MEASURING A TEACHER'S "VALUE-ADDED" TO STUDENT LEARNING

"Value-added" assessment is the tool developed by economists and statisticians to measure and compare teacher quality. The approach uses a statistical model to estimate how a particular student would perform at the end of the year, on average, had she been assigned to one teacher instead of another. The procedure (imperfectly, but, many researchers believe, sufficiently) accounts for factors that each student brings, as well as the resources within the school that are at the teacher's disposal. We can use the results from these analyses to discern how much teacher quality varies under the current system.

Properly conducting value-added analysis requires access to detailed data that follows individual students over time and matches them to their teachers. Administrative data sets of that sort did not exist on a wide scale until the beginning of the twenty-first century, making statistical evaluations of teacher quality impossible. Such data sets are now common and could be universal across the states within the next decade.

Value-added measures rely on a common statistical technique known as multiple regression. Regression measures how differences in an outcome of interest (dependent variable) are related to differences in other factors (independent variables) while holding each of the other input measures constant. Regression is the workhorse of the social sciences: whenever you see note of an empirical social science study, in education or otherwise, there's a good chance that the authors are using some form of a regression. In the case of value-added measures, the regression analysis estimates how differences in observed characteristics about a student, his school, and his teacher are related to changes in his math or reading test scores in a particular year.

Value-added analysis predicts how well a student should perform in a given year based on a series of observable (and sometimes unobservable) factors that are related to his academic achievement but are outside of the teacher's control, such as race, gender, and family income. The analysis then compares for each teacher its estimate of how well her students were expected to perform at the end of the year given the characteristics that they brought into the classroom, to their actual test scores in the spring. Those teachers whose students are performing better than expected will have a positive value-added score, and those teachers whose students are performing worse than expected will have a negative score.

A common complaint about the value-added method is that students walk into a teacher's classroom with varying levels of skill. Accounting for characteristics such as race, ethnicity, and income might help to mitigate such differences, but they don't eliminate them. On average, African American students have lower academic proficiency than white students, but there is wide variation in the performance of students in any racial or ethnic group.

Value-added models control for the ability that students bring by accounting for their test scores at the end of the previous school year. This procedure is common in education policy research and ensures that the model considers factors most related to the child's academic growth. In contrast, the level of his academic achievement is largely determined by outside factors, such as parental influence. Prior student test scores are used to control for several factors that are (1) important to student proficiency at the end of the year, (2) outside of a school's or teacher's control, and (3) cannot be observed by the researcher.

For example, if the student comes from a family that read to him, or if he went to an effective school in prior years, those and similar factors would be reflected in his test scores at the end of the previous year and can be held constant by accounting for it in the statistical model. Some value-added analyses control for two or more previous years of a student's test scores in order to improve the model's ability to hold such unobserved factors constant. Thus the models are constructed to avoid penalizing teachers whose students arrive with low proficiency.

Teacher quality is one factor among many that value-added analyses use to measure student learning, but it is the one we are most concerned with in this book. Properly interpreted, these models tell us the average influence that a teacher has on her students' academic proficiency gains in a year.

We now have several studies using the basic value-added methodology to identify and compare teacher effectiveness. This still-growing body of research demonstrates that there is in fact wide variation in the quality of teachers, even among those who have passed through the system's imposing screens.

2

HOW IMPORTANT ARE TEACHERS?

There are really only two ways that public school teachers are portrayed in popular culture. There is the indefatigable classroom dynamo who single-handedly turns around the lives of her bright but previously neglected students. On the other hand, comedies bring us the doofus teacher who either doesn't care—for example, Steven Colbert's hilarious Mr. Noblet in the cult classic series *Strangers with Candy*—or who, like *South Park*'s Mr. Garrison, are so misguided that they think that episodes of *Barnaby Jones* contain important lessons for a third-grade class.

Many of us love to laugh at the ridiculousness of the bad teachers, and just as many enjoy being inspired by the great teachers on screen. But these characters resonate with us because both are over-the-top versions of reality. Most of us who have found success in life can point to at least one teacher who inspired us. On the other hand, one need not go too far to find examples of teachers who fail to either educate or inspire. Both types of teachers are certainly in the classroom today, along with the majority who are in the middle of these extremes.

Consider this revealing exchange between President Obama and a Philadelphia teacher during an "Open for Questions" town hall meeting at the White House.[1]

President Obama: *How long have you been teaching?*
Philadelphia teacher: *Fifteen years.*
President Obama: *Fifteen years. Okay, so you've been teaching for fifteen years. I'll bet you'll admit that during those fifteen years there have been a couple of teachers that you've met—you don't have to say their names— (laughter)—who you would not put your child in*

13

> *their classroom. (Laughter) See? Right? You're not*
> *saying anything. (Laughter) You're taking the Fifth.*
> *(Laughter) My point is that if we've done everything*
> *we can to improve teacher pay and teacher perfor-*
> *mance and training and development, some people*
> *just aren't meant to be teachers, just like some people*
> *aren't meant to be carpenters, some people aren't*
> *meant to be nurses. At some point they've got to find*
> *a new career.*

President Obama, the audience, and this teacher all *know* that there are some bad teachers in schools today. The uncomfortable laughter in the above exchange occurs only because the president pointed to the elephant in the room that we all politely ignore.

Even the most hardened defenders of the current system's structure observe that there are some teachers who simply don't belong in the classroom. Take the scene of a struggling Chicago public school displayed by Jonathan Kozol in his celebrated book *Savage Inequalities*. Many of the classrooms in the school Kozol toured were headed by uninspired teachers simply going through the motions, and their students were understandably bored and not learning. Some of the teachers hardly show up for work, and when they do they express having very low expectations for their students. The principal explains to Kozol that many of his teachers should have been fired when they moved from their previous position, but are instead assigned to his school. In this same school Kozol finds a classroom dynamo teaching fifth and sixth graders. This teacher engages her students. She has high expectations for the kids, and makes herself available to them and their parents after school hours.[2] Her students were lucky to be assigned to her classroom and not one down the hall.

Such scenes play out each school day in far too many public schools throughout the nation. No one truly believes that all of America's teachers are effective. That's why the first question a concerned parent will ask at the dinner table after the first day of school is, "How's your teacher?" Parents lobby to have their child assigned to or away from particular teachers because they know that a competent and engaged teacher is the key to a successful school year.

We shouldn't be surprised that there are some duds and some superstars among the nation's 3.2 million public school teachers.[3] The same is true in any profession, trade, or job. But it's of tremendous policy importance that we know the extent to which the bad and great teachers are the exception or the rule. Policy makers and parents need to understand just how big a difference it makes for a student to be assigned to one teacher or another. After all, if only a few bad teachers were spread throughout a vast public school system, it would be unfortunate to be sure, but it would be no crisis.

Most of us act as if we understand that there is variation in teacher quality. Ask yourself: Would you support a policy that assigned your child's teacher randomly? When considering your answer, don't just think of the teachers in your child's school—many people reading this book will have moved into a neighborhood specifically because of its high-performing schools and high-quality teachers—but think of randomly assigning your child any teacher who works in that specific grade from any school district in the state. If you believe that teachers are essentially the same, you should be perfectly comfortable with that lottery. You must then believe that the chance your child gets one of the system's few duds is quite small. If that strikes you as a gamble that you'd rather not take, then you believe that teacher quality varies enough to be a concern.

Only two decades ago, it was impossible to quantify the variation in teacher quality. Principals and teachers have always been able to identify the best and worst teachers in their school. But how much better is Mrs. Johnson than Mr. Smith? How many great teachers are there? How many duds? There were previously no tools available capable of measuring the difference in learning outcomes that occur when a student is assigned to one or another teacher.

The empirical revolution that has overtaken education in the past several years has dramatically improved our knowledge about the quality of public school teachers. Though imperfect, the quantitative tools described in the previous chapter provide us with estimates of just how wide and meaningful the variation in teacher quality is in our public school classrooms.

In one sense, the wide body of empirical research produced over the last several years only confirms and quantifies what parents, policy makers, school administrators, and teachers themselves have always suspected: some teachers are great, most are doing fine, and there are some teachers whose students fall far behind. What's surprising and important is just how big the difference in teacher quality actually is, and just how many failing teachers there are throughout every school system.

WHAT VARIATION IN TEACHER QUALITY?

The most fundamental assumption on which the current system is based is that teachers are not dramatically different from one another once we account for their credentials and experience. On the surface, there seems to be some good reasons to believe that assumption. The current system provides a series of screens and requirements that are intended to keep the variation in teacher quality to a minimum.

The foundation of our belief in relative teacher equality is that they are required to complete a minimal level of training in an education college before they enter the classroom. We assume that prospective teachers are learning the techniques they need in order to effectively manage classrooms along with the content knowledge they need to express to students. Anyone who possesses those skills, most assume, should have the tools to become an effective teacher.

No one expects that all graduates of a teaching program are identically effective in the classroom any more than they suspect that every law school graduate is equally capable of presenting oral arguments before the Supreme Court. But the degree requirement should ensure that a teacher has met some minimal standard, and thus few, if any, teachers should enter the classroom terribly unprepared. The training requirement serves as an important barrier to entering the public school teaching workforce and should provide meaningful quality control.

Teachers also receive several certifications and licensures that are meant to ensure that they meet at least some minimal standard. Teachers receive general licenses as well as certifications in specific subjects. To earn these credentials teachers must either pass an exam or have completed a necessary set of course work. The certification requirement in theory ensures that each public school teacher has been deemed by the state and an institution of higher learning to have met a minimum threshold for quality.

Many teachers also acquire additional credentials. More than half of public school teachers working today have earned at least a master's degree.[4] Parents expect that a teacher who has earned an advanced degree has the expertise necessary to far surpass a minimal threshold for classroom effectiveness.

A proper credentialing process can ensure teacher quality in at least two ways. Most obviously, it excludes those who fail to achieve a minimal standard for a teaching profession. Additionally, imposing certain hurdles has an influence on the type of person who enters the profession in the first place.

For example, closing the profession to people who have not graduated with an education degree will keep out those who see teaching as a brief escapade rather than a career. Spending four years in a specialized education program rather than earning general liberal arts or science degree serves as a signal to school systems (that is, prospective employers) that the aspiring teacher is interested in the profession for the long term.

Consider Jane, a talented college freshman with high SAT scores and a magnetic personality who is considering a major in education or business law. Jane finds the idea of working with kids to be very appealing. She is a person of high ideals who wants to help disadvantaged students reach their potential. However, she doesn't see teaching as her only career. Since she was a little girl she has dreamed of becoming a lawyer and she plans to go to law school after about five years in the working world. Jane is willing to give teaching a try—perhaps she will love it!—but she decides that the five years or so she imagines herself teaching don't justify her replacing her generally useful business courses with courses in pedagogy and classroom management.

The current thinking in the educational system is perfectly happy that Jane has decided not to become a teacher. It values only 100 percent commitment to teaching, perhaps because we assume that teachers who see teaching as a lifelong career will be more dedicated to their students and that a teacher's effectiveness increases with years of experience.

Nor does the current public school system particularly like the idea of Jane taking a stab at teaching after she has graduated college with a degree other than education. Though she is a smart and dedicated young woman, we act on the assumption that without the instruction in pedagogical practices, classroom-management techniques, and the social justification for teaching, Jane won't have acquired the specific technical skills necessary for classroom success.

Of course, graduating from an education college doesn't ensure that Jane would make great teacher. There will be some variation in teacher quality even if the screens imposed are effective at keeping out unprepared teachers. But if they work properly, the screens should minimize the number of disastrous classroom teachers. It is reasonable to expect that the strong screens used by the current teaching profession should keep the variation in teacher quality relatively small and ensure that nearly all students are matched with teachers who meet at least an adequate standard.

MEASURING TEACHER QUALITY

So, how much does teacher quality actually vary? If, by teacher quality, you refer to earned credentials from accredited institutions, it doesn't vary dramatically. By that definition we can improve teacher quality by both increasing the restriction that prospective teachers earn a teaching certification before they enter a classroom, and by making it more difficult to earn those degrees.

It is tempting to say that a high-quality teacher is well versed in the material taught and has received certain credentials that indicate the skills necessary to succeed in the classroom. In fact, this is precisely how No Child Left Behind, the federal education law, defines a "highly qualified teacher." According to the law, such distinguished teachers "must have: (1) a bachelor's degree, (2) full state certification or licensure, and (3) proof that they know each subject they teach."[5]

Defining a high-quality teacher as one who possesses certain observed attributes fits well into the paradigm that has dominated education policy for decades. We can be sure that a teacher who has checked the necessary boxes is well qualified for the classroom, because that's what the boxes are for! A teacher who has earned a degree and certification from a college of education has demonstrated possession of the body of knowledge thought to be necessary for high-quality teaching. The system operates as if overcoming hurdles to becoming a teacher is not only a necessary but also a sufficient condition for high-quality teaching.

However, a *highly qualified* teacher is no more likely to be a *high-quality* teacher than someone who passes the bar exam is likely to be an effective lawyer.

It is quite odd to define teacher quality by pointing only to a teacher's credentials and experience. Attributes such as certification may (or may not) contribute to a teacher's quality, but they do not define it. We do not care about certification, subject knowledge, pedagogical practices, and so on for their own sake, but rather because we assume that they are important to explaining the teacher's effectiveness in the classroom. In other words, it is not a teacher's inputs that matter—it's her output.

A teacher's effectiveness is defined by his independent contribution to student learning. Deriving the definition of teacher quality entirely from student learning means that we can use the ideas of teacher quality, productivity, and effectiveness interchangeably.

The output-based approach to understanding teacher quality is not often seriously disputed. Advocates of the current system, for example, argue that we must ensure that all teachers are certified because only those teachers who have undergone minimal training are likely to have the skills necessary to teach students effectively. Whether such credentials actually signal that a teacher is effective is an empirical question worth answering. How impressed should you be that your child's new teacher has a master's degree? Do you need to know anything else about her in order to feel comfortable that your child will learn all that she can in that classroom?

Acknowledging that teachers should be judged on their contribution to student learning has consequences. Most importantly, we must give priority to student achievement. Are students assigned to better-credentialed teachers learning more than students assigned to teachers with lesser credentials? If credentialing ensures teacher quality, we would expect the answer to be yes.

THE VARIATION IN TEACHER QUALITY

How much should you worry if your child is assigned to Ms. Smith or Mr. Johnson down the hall? Quite a lot.

Research using the value-added approach consistently finds that teacher quality is the most important factor (within a school's control) for boosting student performance. Students with nearly identical backgrounds will perform quite differently on standardized tests depending on which teacher they were assigned.

An early evaluation of teacher quality provides a representative example of the existing research. In this study, economist Eric Hanushek estimated that a student assigned to a teacher who ranked in the twenty-fifth percentile in quality would have his reading proficiency increase by about half a grade level during the school year, holding all other factors about the student constant.[6] If that same student had been assigned to a teacher at the seventy-fifth percentile in quality, he would have gained a grade-and-a-half's worth of reading proficiency during the school year. That is, the difference between being assigned to one of the system's best teachers and one of its worst is about an additional grade-level's worth of proficiency at the end of the school year. Similar variations in teacher quality have been found in Tennessee,[7] New Jersey,[8] Chicago,[9] Florida,[10] and other unnamed school districts across the country.

Students who are assigned to a great teacher make large academic progress during the school year. When a student is assigned to a bad teacher, he loses substantial academic ground relative to his peers. Those unlucky students who are assigned to a bad teacher two or three years in a row stand little chance of recovering from the damage.

The influence of teacher quality dwarfs that of most other considerations that are within a school's control. For instance, a recent study of public schools in Texas found that a one-standard-deviation increase in the quality of a student's teacher had the same positive impact as reducing class size by about 10 percent.[11]

Research on the variation in teacher quality is ongoing and growing. We still do not know everything about the quality of teachers, and researchers are engaged in vigorous debates over what models should be used to measure teacher effectiveness. Not only articles but recently entire conferences, books, and journal volumes are dedicated to testing the assumptions underlying the measurement of teacher quality.[12]

However, the dust in the air should not blind us. These measurement issues are important, to be sure, especially when we consider how such evaluations might be used to evaluate the performance of individual teachers, as we do in the next chapter. Nonetheless, for the purposes of understanding whether the variation in teacher quality is real or imagined, these statistical issues are largely on the periphery. The lesson of this research is consistent and powerful: teacher quality is the most important element in the classroom, and its variation is vast. Even those who stand strongest in favor of the current system agree with these basic facts. When the American Federation of Teachers declares on its website, "Research findings demonstrate that teacher quality is the single most important school variable affecting student achievement,"[13] they are pointing precisely to the research discussed above.

If teachers weren't important, we could put anyone in the classroom and expect similar results. If teachers weren't important, you should be willing to have your child randomly assigned to any teacher in his school. Modern research leaves no reasonable doubt that the quality of classroom teachers differs dramatically both across and within schools. It turns out that whether your child is assigned to Ms. Smith or Mr. Johnson down the hall is quite a big deal indeed: it could plausibly mean a difference of your child achieving an additional full grade level's worth of learning by the end of the school year.

WHAT FACTORS ARE RELATED TO TEACHER QUALITY?

How much does it matter if your child's teacher graduated from an education college? How impressed should you be if he earned a master's degree?

The fact that there exists wide variation in teacher quality presents the possibility that we could identify factors that are related to teaching effectiveness. Perhaps there are characteristics shared by the most-effective teachers and missing from the least-effective teachers. If there are attributes that help to predict whether a teacher will be effective in a classroom, we could feasibly develop more successful screens than those used currently. Unfortunately, few, if any, such characteristics exist.

Much of the research evaluating teacher quality is focused on the amount of classroom experience and advanced degrees earned. As we will discuss in a later chapter, those are the two factors that determine a teacher's salary.

Economists Eric Hanushek and Steven Rivkin recently surveyed the existing research on the relationship between earning a master's degree and the impact a teacher has on student proficiency.[14] They found no such evidence—literally. Not a single one of the thirty-four studies on the issue that could be deemed "high quality" found that teachers with a master's degree were more effective in the classroom than teachers without one.

The empirical research on classroom experience isn't much more encouraging than the work on credentials. Research does in fact find a positive relationship between the number of years a teacher has spent in the classroom and her influence on student achievement. But most of this work finds that the benefits of experience plateaus after the third to fifth year. The average teacher is at her worst during the first year in the classroom, gets better in the second year, a little better in her third year, and then she never gets any better after that.

It is important to keep in mind that quantitative research measures the average influence of teacher characteristics on classroom effectiveness. The research does not say that no teachers improve after five years in the classroom, and some teachers certainly do benefit from what they learn when earning an advanced degree. However, the evidence is clear that those factors are not intrinsically related to improvements in teacher quality. The fact that years of experience and credentials, on average, do not influence a teacher's effectiveness is of enormous policy importance.

More finely tuned measures of a teacher's attributes also seem to show little relationship to teacher quality. Whether a teacher is certified does not seem to predict whether he will be effective in the classroom.[15] A more recent strand of research looking at the relationship between the courses that teachers take in college and the academic achievement of the teacher's students also fails to find much of an effect.[16] Even measures of intelligence, such as their score on the SAT exam, are only slightly related to a teacher's contribution to student learning.[17]

Even to the limited extent to which they might be related to student achievement, observed characteristics about the teacher's training, experience, and cognitive ability explain remarkably little of a teacher's contribution to student learning. Typically, research suggests that *about 3 percent* of the teacher's contribution to his students' math and reading scores can be explained by factors that are typically collected in an administrative data set.[18] That is, upwards of 97 percent of what makes one teacher more effective than another is unrelated to factors such as the number of years he has been teaching, the credentials he has earned, and even performance on vocabulary tests. It turns out that learning that your child's teacher has ten years of experience and a master's degree doesn't tell you very much at all about the amount you can expect your child to learn in his class.

Most of what makes one teacher better than another has to do with innate personal characteristics. In a recent study of new teachers in New York City, a group of well-known researchers surveyed teachers on a variety of cognitive and noncogitative characteristics such as measures of their conscientiousness and extraversion. Consistent with prior research, they found that conventional measures, such as the earning of advanced degrees, were unrelated to the teacher's classroom effectiveness. On their own, the more detailed measures of a teacher's personality characteristics were generally unrelated to performance, but they did help to predict a teacher's effectiveness when considered in tandem. However, even with this very detailed information about a teacher's personality—information that public schools do not generally collect—the authors were able to explain only a small portion of the variance in teacher quality. They concluded that considering such unconventional measures could improve upon current teacher recruitment efforts, but that their result "underscores the difficult, perhaps impossible task of identifying systematically the most highly effective or ineffective teachers without any data on actual performance in the classroom."[19]

The clear way to interpret the research is that the vast majority of what makes a teacher effective derives from factors that are not easily observed before the teacher stands in front of a classroom. Perhaps that result is not as surprising at it first appears. Attributes like the teacher's patience, enthusiasm, presence in the classroom, and the ability to recognize when students are following the material and when they are falling behind are almost certainly critical to success, but such personal factors are innate to the individual and thus largely not learned in a college of education or dramatically improved upon after three to five years of experience.

THE LESSON FROM MODERN RESEARCH

The large variation in teacher effectiveness is strong evidence that the screens currently in place are ineffective. Clearly, we have more than a few poorly performing teachers even though just about everyone had to pass through a screening process before they started teaching.

According to Hanushek's estimates from Texas, the system's best teachers are making dramatic improvements in their students' academic achievement, but about one in four teachers are covering half a year or less of material in their classrooms, after accounting for the students' background characteristics and prior achievement.

We know that teachers are important, and it is clear that they vary dramatically in effectiveness. We also know that we have no way of predicting how well a teacher will perform in the classroom based on observed factors such as training, experience, intelligence, or anything else for that matter. Those basic facts point us toward a very different system than the one in operation today.

A system that uses screens to ensure minimal levels of teacher quality presupposes that individuals who pass through the screens are more effective in the classroom than those who do not. From a policy maker's perspective, it isn't even necessary that prospective teachers actually benefit from their time enrolled in an education program or when obtaining the training necessary for particular certifications. What it required, however, is that those who manage to pass through the screens are generally more effective than those who do not. If they do not distinguish between effective and ineffective teachers, then the screens developed by the current system are meaningless wastes of time and resources.

The fact that what makes one teacher better than another is not well described by their training, experience, or any other easily observed characteristic has enormous consequences. These empirical findings mean that not only are the screens used by the current system inadequate, but also that there is little chance that they could be replaced with more-effective screens. We might be able to improve upon our current methods, but we stand little chance of accurately identifying the best and worst teachers before they enter the classroom.

A more-effective system would observe a teacher's effectiveness, weed out the poorly performing teachers, and retain the highly effective teachers. Considering our inability to use observed characteristics about teacher to predict how well they perform in the classroom, currently we have the procedure exactly backward.

Clearly, the variation in teacher quality is meaningful enough to command our attention. Addressing the variation in teacher quality requires us to use systems capable of identifying the most- and least-effective teachers and then act upon such information in such a way that we remove bad teachers and retain effective teachers. The current system is woefully inadequate for those enormously important jobs.

The variation in teacher quality is a direct result of our employment relationship with public school teachers. The root issue is that we employ teachers based entirely on characteristics that are unrelated to their effectiveness and brazenly ignore their actual contribution to student learning. In the past, such a system was perhaps inevitable because information about teacher quality was scarce. The newly available information, however, makes this system intolerable.

3

HOW DO WE IDENTIFY
EFFECTIVE TEACHERS?

Step one toward improving teacher quality is to identify which teachers are effective and which are not. A reliable evaluation system is also the bedrock on which teacher quality reform must be built. We cannot hope to make informed decisions about which teachers deserve tenure, which teachers have earned salary increases, which teachers need help from their peers, and even which teachers should be removed from the classroom unless we first have a system for differentiating between those who are successful and those who are not. Our current system for evaluating teachers doesn't fit the bill. The American public school system is only now beginning to take this challenge seriously.

Modern research confirms what everyone suspected: teachers are enormously important to student learning, and some teachers are much more effective than others. The only people who seem to believe that all public school teachers are equally effective are the administrators who evaluate them. Believe it or not, nearly all public school teachers receive the same positive rating on their official evaluations.

The problem of uniformly positive teacher evaluations is well known by policy makers. Early in his tenure as US secretary of education, Arne Duncan summarized the issue well when he lamented to a group of education researchers, "In California, they have 300,000 teachers. If you took the top 10 percent, they have 30,000 of the best teachers in the world. If you took the bottom 10 percent, they have 30,000 teachers that should probably find another profession, yet no one in California can tell you which teacher is in which category. Something is wrong with that picture."[1]

On its face, an evaluation system that fails to distinguish between a teacher who is pushing her students to new academic heights and a teacher who sends her students to the next grade without having taught them half of what was expected in a given year is worse than useless.

The data revolution provides an important tool that we can use to improve teacher evaluations. As we saw in the previous chapter, widespread standardized testing and the development of the value-added methodology allow us to estimate a teacher's independent contribution to student learning. While we should not use test-score analysis in isolation, it can and should supplement qualitative teacher evaluations as conformation of how much a teacher's students are learning.

Nowhere is the data and information revolution more essential for public education than in identifying effective and ineffective teachers. If we are to address the variation in teacher quality, we must first develop an evaluation system capable of distinguishing between the best and worst teachers. No evaluation tool is perfect. But improving teacher quality requires first taking seriously the important job of identifying those teachers who are effective and those teachers who are not.

ALL TEACHERS ARE EFFECTIVE

If both empirical evidence and our own experiences tell us that there is wide variation in teacher quality, why is just about everyone teaching in an American public school rated to be an effective teacher according to their official evaluations?

The New Teacher Project analyzed the results of teacher evaluations in twelve large school districts across four states. They found that in districts using a binary evaluation system (meaning there are only two ratings: "satisfactory" or "not satisfactory"), more than 99 percent of teachers received the thumbs-up rating. Even districts that used broader evaluation distinctions ranked 94 percent of teachers in one of the top two tiers of effectiveness and deemed just 1 percent of them "unsatisfactory."[2]

There might be some great schools in which all of the teachers are effective. But the struggles of urban school systems, in particular, make it impossible to take universally positive teacher evaluations seriously.

According to the results of the National Assessment of Educational Progress—a highly respected test administered to representative samples of students each year by the US Department of Education and commonly referred to as the Nation's Report Card—in 2007 only 57 percent of fourth graders in New York City and 44 percent of fourth graders in Chicago could "demonstrate an understanding of the overall meaning of what they read. When reading text appropriate for fourth graders they are able to make relatively obvious connections between the text and their own experiences and extend the ideas in the text by making simple inferences."[3] Even considering that urban students come to school facing greater difficulties than do students in more-affluent communities, such low student proficiency suggests that at least some teachers aren't particularly effective in the classroom. And yet, that same year less than 2 percent of New York's fifty-six thousand classroom teachers[4] and less than one percent of Chicago's nineteen thousand teachers[5] were deemed "unsatisfactory" on their official evaluations. Most teachers were rated well above par: During the period from 2003 to 2006, 61 percent of teachers in Chicago received the highest rating on the evaluation ("superior"); 32 percent were rated "excellent"; and the remaining 7 percent were still considered "satisfactory."[6]

Teachers receive uniformly positive evaluations even in the worst schools in urban districts. As in other urban school districts, only 3.4 percent of Houston's public school teachers ranked "below expectations" or "unsatisfactory" on their evaluations from 2005–2006 through 2008–2009. Even more discouraging, an analysis by The New Teacher Project discovered that only 2 of the 661 teachers working in schools formally recognized by the Houston Independent School District as "academically unacceptable" ranked unsatisfactorily on any single component of their official evaluation.[7] Yet 45 percent of Houston's public school fourth graders scored below the Basic level on NAEP in 2009.

New York City's example shows just how challenging is the task of identifying ineffective teachers. In 2009–2010, only 2.29 percent of New York City's teachers received an "unsatisfactory" rating on their official evaluation. Few if anyone working in the city's public schools would tell you that more than 97 percent of the teachers are effective. Nonetheless, that shockingly low identification rate of poorly performing Gotham teachers actually represents an enormous improvement in the evaluation system: As early as 2005–2006, only 0.89 percent of New York City's teachers were deemed "unsatisfactory."

The increases in the percentage of teachers deemed to be poor performing in New York City is both more impressive and disheartening when considered in the larger historical context. A 1914 study of New York City's teacher evaluation system found that only 0.5 percent of teachers evaluated in New York City were considered deficient in instruction and only 0.9 percent were considered nonmeritorious in discipline.[8] Uniformly positive teacher ratings were no easier to believe in the early twentieth century than they are today. The study's author lambasted the evaluation system and blamed the homogeneity in teacher evaluation results on extremely low standards for effectiveness. A century later, we still do not distinguish between effective and ineffective teachers.

Historically, public schools have never taken teacher evaluations seriously. Rubber-stamping teachers' performance is a long-standing problem that even predates collective bargaining and influential teachers' unions.

Perhaps better than anyone, teachers themselves understand that some of their colleagues receive performance ratings that they don't deserve. A survey of four large urban school systems revealed that 58 percent of teachers believe that there is at least one tenured teacher in their school who poorly instructs students, and 43 percent of teachers believe that there is at least one tenured teacher in their school whose performance is so poor that they should be removed from the classroom. Public school teachers in Chicago pointed to 8 percent of their colleagues when they were asked to identify poor-performing teachers in their own schools. But the variation in teacher quality is not in any way captured in the current performance evaluation process: recall that less than 1 percent of Chicago's teachers receive an "unsatisfactory" rating each year.

The homogenous results of teacher evaluations provide a clear illustration of the most fundamental issue with teacher quality in the public schools: everyone believes that teachers are important, and yet, the current system treats all teachers as if they are identical.

PRIORITIZING TEACHER OUTPUTS

The primary reason evaluations fail to provide useful information about how well a teacher contributes to her students' learning is that they aren't meant to do so. The current system prioritizes process and credentials rather than student achievement, either in quantitative or qualitative terms.

To most people, it would be an uncontroversial to assert that a teacher's value derives from whether or not her students are learning. A good teacher is one who contributes substantially to his students' learning, and a bad teacher is one who contributes to student learning very little. It's odd, then, that public school systems do not base any part of a teacher's evaluation on whether the teacher contributes to student achievement.

The case for focusing on teacher outputs rather than credentials is so obvious that it shouldn't need to be discussed. If the purpose of a school is to foster student learning, then a successful teacher is one whose students show measurable improvement. How a teacher reaches or fails to reach that goal (within parameters, of course) is a secondary concern, if it is a concern at all.

Think back to the three teachers in whose classes you learned the most during your time in school. Did they all follow the same protocol? Did they have the same credentials? Now think of a few teachers in whose class students struggled. Those teachers may have been well-meaning and have pursued pedagogical strategies learned in education colleges. But for some reason you may not have learned in their classrooms.

Of course, some classroom techniques are generally more effective than others. Prioritizing classroom outputs does not mean that we should completely eliminate consideration of the teacher's techniques. A protocol of best practices could be very useful for beginning teachers or for teachers who are struggling. Teachers could benefit from expansive research and development on the sorts of classroom techniques that tend to help students the most.

In fact, a promising movement toward improving teacher development is well underway. This movement is not occurring within the education colleges, but despite them. The people at Teach for America have leveraged into a guide for teacher training their two decades of experience recruiting, training, and evaluating teachers from America's most competitive universities.[9] Doug Lemov, cofounder of the Network of Uncommon Schools—schools that have been working miracles with inner-city kids across the nation—has been crisscrossing the country providing seminars on the attributes and classroom-management techniques used by some of his most effective teachers.[10] If every teacher in America followed the advice of these reformers then surely teacher quality in our public schools would dramatically improve.

But even the best tools can be imperfectly or even improperly used in the classroom. For instance, as we will discuss further in a later chapter, though Teach for America teachers are generally more effective than their more experienced colleagues who were trained in colleges of education, there remains wide variation in their effectiveness despite the fact that each is a graduate of the program's famous Teacher U.

There is no foolproof protocol for teaching any more than there is a failsafe method of shooting free throws in basketball. Most players who learn the proper technique to shoot a foul shot become reasonably effective shooters. But there will always be those players for whom the conventional technique doesn't work so well. Some players develop their own successful shooting strategies. Some players, like Shaq, simply lack the touch to ever become a successful foul shooter. Still others will simply ignore the instruction all together and shoot poorly.

Evaluations should largely depend on the extent to which the teacher contributes to student learning, not the extent to which she is following a particular protocol—even if it's a much better protocol than exists today. If it is student learning that we care about, then it is student learning that should garner our primary attention when we evaluate teachers. If we believe that very basic premise, then we must consider a far different evaluation tool than is currently in place in most school districts.

WHY THE CURRENT SYSTEM FAILS TO IDENTIFY TEACHER EFFECTIVENESS

One of the major reasons evaluations are routinely inflated is because the evaluators face only costs and no benefits for correctly identifying an ineffective teacher.

Classroom observation is the primary tool used in most teacher-evaluation systems. In a typical observation, the school's principal and sometimes a group of other evaluators sit in on a teacher's classroom session and rate him, often according to a defined protocol. The evaluator rates the teacher's performance according to a limited scale—for example, "satisfactory" or "unsatisfactory"—based on several aspects of the teacher's classroom management techniques.[11]

Observations are attractive in several ways. They provide principals with some direct experience with the teacher that could help direct future interactions together. For an experienced and insightful observer, they also allow an opportunity to identify not only the fact that a teacher is indeed struggling, but also which individual aspects of his approach might be improved.

However, while observations are important, they are insufficient—even when they are carried out with good faith and by competent evaluators.

Currently, classroom observations are far too infrequent to be informative. Recently hired, untenured teachers are often observed annually, and even up to two to three times a year. But principals rarely observe the performance of teachers who have been in the classroom for a few years. A US Department of Education study of teacher evaluations in the Midwest found that in more than half the districts studied, tenured teachers were only evaluated once every three years.[12] In Chicago, tenured teachers whose last rating was "Excellent" or "Superior"—recall, those ratings accounted for 93 percent of evaluations in Chicago between 2003 and 2006—are evaluated every two years.[13] In Los Angeles—another consistently struggling urban school system—tenured teachers who have been in the district for at least ten years and meet the conditions to be considered "highly qualified" need not be evaluated more than once every three to five years.[14]

Even in the years that teachers are observed in the classroom, their principals spend very little time on the process. In the very low-performing Miami-Dade school system, the required annual official observation need not last longer than twenty minutes.[15] In its study of teacher evaluations in Arkansas, Colorado, Illinois, and Ohio, the New Teacher Project found tenured teachers were observed for an average of seventy-five minutes during the school year. Nor do principals spend time evaluating novice teachers: the New Teacher Project survey found probationary teachers were evaluated for an average of eighty-one minutes in a school year.

A teacher's job is far too complex for observations once every three years—or even a couple times a year—to judge their performance soundly. How does the teacher help students who are struggling? How well does she handle disorderly behavior? Can she keep students engaged over long periods and when covering difficult material? Those are all important factors that determine how much students learn by the end of the year and are questions one would want to answer when deciding whether a teacher is meeting expectations, needs to improve, or should be let go. No matter how appropriate the protocol or how astute the evaluator, these and other important questions simply cannot be answered by watching her teach a single class period or less once every year or so.

Exacerbating the problem is the fact that the current system is not open to truly identifying those teachers who are ineffective. Teachers expect to receive the highest ratings only because experience tells them virtually all of their peers are rated that way. Furthermore, pressures outside of the classroom serve to punish principals who identify ineffective teachers, while offering no rewards for the trouble.

Principals are, in fact, capable of identifying the most- and least-effective teachers in their school. A recent study found that principals who were asked to rate their teachers on a scale from 1 (inadequate) to 10 (exceptional) were very good at identifying those teachers who are the best and worst performing according to their value-added contribution to student test scores—the top and bottom 20 percent in their school—according to measures of the influence a teacher has on his student's test scores.[16] Even with such limited classroom observations, it's obvious from daily behavior and the word in the hallways which teachers are failing. It's an open secret that everyone in a school knows who is effective and who isn't.

Principals are well aware that the uniformly positive ratings that they dole out to their teachers are more than somewhat bogus. More than half (56 percent) of veteran Chicago principals reported in a survey that they assigned higher evaluations to teachers than they thought were warranted.[17] In contrast to the high satisfactory rates they give teachers on official evaluations, only 46 percent of a random sample of principals nationwide said that the teachers in their school were "excellent."[18] Principals routinely give teachers high ratings that they don't deserve in large part because failing a teacher on an evaluation creates headaches but brings little if any tangible reward.

The current system embeds explicit policies that make it difficult for a principal to give a poor rating to a teacher. Collective bargaining agreements routinely afford teachers powerful means to fight back if they do not agree with their evaluation. In Los Angeles, a teacher who is identified as exhibiting "below standard performance" may file a grievance according to the rules of the union contract.[19]

The difficulty that principals face when they give a teacher anything but the highest mark proves to be a powerful incentive to inflate a bad teacher's rating. Of those veteran Chicago principals who had admitted on a survey that they assigned teachers higher ratings than they deserved, more than half cited as a reason that the union contract restricts their ability to lower a teacher's rating. A third of these principals said that giving the teachers an accurate rating wasn't worth engaging in a lengthy grievance process.[20]

Avoiding paperwork isn't a good excuse for an administrator keeping bad teachers in the classroom. But then again, giving a teacher a bad rating is unrelated to her remaining in front of students: principals can afford to dole out uniformly positive marks because today's evaluations have no meaningful consequences for teachers after they have managed to stay in the classroom for a few years.

As we will see in a later chapter, tenured teachers are insulated by a series of job protections that make them nearly impossible to fire or even sanction. In most cases a principal can't remove an ineffective teacher no matter how unsatisfactory her rating. Of those Chicago principals who admitted that they inflated their evaluations, 30 percent said they did so in part because giving a low rating wasn't worth the trouble since they could not dismiss the teacher anyway.[21]

Not only do teacher evaluations fail to initiate a teacher's firing, teacher-performance ratings are so meaningless that they don't even come into play when a school district is forced to let some teachers go. As we will discuss further in a later chapter, collective bargaining agreements, and in some cases state law, mandate that when a school district is forced to lay off teachers for budgetary reasons, seniority is the only factor that can be taken into consideration. Thus, the rare distinction of an unsatisfactory rating plays no role in determining whether a poorly performing teacher is removed from the classroom—even when the school system is forced to fire that teacher's higher-performing peers.

We might suspect that giving a bad teacher a poor rating could be a motivational tool, or could lead to interventions by peer teachers and administrators in an attempt to help the teacher get better. But the rarity with which poor evaluations are issued reduces their motivational properties and tends to further reduce a principal's willingness to use the designation. Instead, a poor rating implies that the recipient is not only "unsatisfactory" but is egregiously incompetent: Roughly three in one thousand Chicago public school teachers are rated "unsatisfactory" each year, and thus such a rating would imply that the teacher performs worse than 99.97 percent of her colleagues in this poor-performing school system.[22] That's often a much stronger message than a principal intends to send. The principal is left with no way to distinguish on his or her official evaluation between an ineffective teacher who could use some remediation and a hapless one who should find a new career. The default becomes to just list the teacher's performance as satisfactory or higher.

The "unsatisfactory" rating is a distinction embarrassing enough to fight with powerful weapons but too meaningless for an administrator to defend. Given the many factors standing in the way, it's a wonder that any teachers are rated "unsatisfactory" at all.

Classroom observations and the discretion of principals should play a meaningful role in evaluating teachers. But the current task is far too weighty for today's evaluations given their limitations. If evaluations are to be meaningful then their results must have stakes, and we need to use tools capable of distinguishing the most- and least-effective teachers.

HOW SHOULD PUBLIC SCHOOLS EVALUATE THEIR TEACHERS?

A rich evaluation system would use a combination of objective and subjective measures to evaluate a teacher's overall contribution to his students' learning. It would rate teachers largely based on their performance in the classroom, yet be capable of identifying untapped potential and providing recommendations for improvement.

Student learning should be at the center of teacher evaluations. Public schools should utilize the best measure of a teacher's contribution to student learning that we have available: quantitative analysis in the form of value-added assessment.

INTRODUCING QUANTITATIVE MEASURES
IN TEACHER EVALUATIONS

Less than even a decade ago, schools lacked real objective student-performance measures that might have been used to evaluate teachers. Students received scores on tests and accumulated a grade point average, but those measures did not provide uniform meaning among schools or even among classrooms within a school. A teacher heading a classroom filled with "A" students might be very effective, or just an easy grader.[23] Thus, previous teacher evaluations could not have depended on quantitative analysis even if school systems were inclined to go in that direction.

The quantitative and scientific revolution in education policy has brought with it the tools and procedures necessary to objectively evaluate teachers across a school system. Value-added analysis takes into account both observed and unobserved factors related to a student's test score and should be used to inform—*not replace*—teacher evaluations.

New York City, the nation's largest school district, provides an example of how quantitative analysis can be used to improve teacher evaluations. In 2009, it began creating reports based on value-added analyses of the three-year performance of a teacher's students on the state's mandated math and reading exams. The four-page report compares the teacher's measured impact on her students to those of teachers citywide and to a select group of teachers whose classrooms had similar demographics.

The objectivity inherent in statistical techniques is one of value-added assessment's most attractive features. Proper analysis of student test scores doesn't take into account whether the teacher is likely to file a grievance if given a poor rating. The computer carrying out the estimation doesn't care if school solidarity is threatened by pointing out that the bad teacher who everyone knows is a bad teacher is in fact a bad teacher. All the analysis knows is that a student who enters into a teacher's classroom at the beginning of the year tends to leave it at the end of the year with a higher or lower proficiency level than is expected given the demographic to which he belongs and his previous performance. That is, value-added assessment treats each teacher equally and focuses sharply on what we care about most.

Analysis of student test-score growth also has the advantage of evaluating overall teacher performance as it relates to student math and reading proficiency rather than just limited observations of it. Even at their best, classroom observations can only give a glance of the teacher's actions. No matter how astute, the observer cannot possibly judge every aspect of the teacher's performance. Test-score analysis, on the other hand, focuses on the end product of the school year, and thus takes into account each classroom day.

Just as they would enhance the school system's identification of a teacher's effectiveness, evaluations using information from value-added models also improve the feedback that teachers receive about their own performance. A teacher learns nothing about her effectiveness in the classroom from her "satisfactory" rating when it is the same mark all other teachers in her school receive. In addition, a consideration of her students' raw test scores can provide a teacher with misleading information about her contribution to student learning. A young teacher working with disadvantaged students might become disheartened by the fact that her students score low on standardized tests relative to other students in the state. By zeroing in on the teacher's own contribution to her students' learning, value-added assessment provides good teachers with the knowledge that they are doing something right.

It is a national scandal that so few school districts have adopted real evaluations. Information is the key to good decision making. Even if it is imperfect, why would we throw away generally reliable information about the quality of our teachers?

And the research demonstrates that even this imperfect information provides far better measures of teacher quality than are currently employed. A recent analysis by economists Dan Goldhaber and Michael Hansen found that a teacher's value-added score from her performance in the first three years in the classroom is a significant predictor of the achievement of her students during her fifth school year.[24] On the other hand, similar to the findings of several other studies, they found that conventional measures of teacher quality—years of experience, college selectivity, licensure status, and whether the teacher held a master's degree—are unrelated to student learning in the teacher's fifth classroom year.

FAIR FOR WHOM?

Despite the advantages, there are still many who believe that the limitations inherent in test-score analysis are undermining the benefits.

They emphasize that the results of value-added models are never entirely accurate measures of the teacher's contribution to student learning. Since value-added is a statistical tool, its estimates will always be influenced by random error.

No statistical model can account for every factor that produces a student's test score at the end of the year. Even more worrisome is the fact that seemingly random factors contribute to student test scores. Student scores might fluctuate if the paragraph used in a reading comprehension question on the exam happened to be based on something the student knows a lot about, or if there was a dog barking outside of the classroom window distracting students when they were taking the exam, or if a few kids guessed right on some questions in one teacher's classroom and happened to guess wrong in another teacher's classroom, and so on. The ramification of random error—or what researchers often refer to as "noise"—is that it will always be the case that some good teachers will appear to have low value-added and some bad teachers will score better than they should.

The problem of random error in value-added assessment can lead to what seem to be quite imprecise measures of teacher quality. Most studies find that test-score measures of a teacher's value-added correlate from one year to the next at a rate of between 0.30 and 0.40. The implication is that there is substantial variability in the measure of an individual teacher's effectiveness from one year to the next.

The variability in teacher ratings based on value-added analysis is large enough to produce some disheartening data. For instance, only about a third of teachers with value-added scores ranking in the bottom or top quartiles in one year will rank in those same quartiles the next year. It is observed that many teachers will have gone from ranking near the bottom to near the top, and vice versa. Some of these differences in a teacher's year-to-year value-added score almost certainly have to do with actual changes in the teacher's classroom behavior—that is, the teacher might actually perform differently from year to year. But some, likely large, portion of the variability is due to random error.

The influence of random factors decreases as more observation is included in the analysis, and thus the validity increases as a given teacher is observed over more years, and with more students. The consequence is that value-added estimates cannot be based on a single year's worth of data. Analyses based on at least two years of matching students to teachers are useful. Those based on three or more years are preferable. Nonetheless, even evaluations using multiple years of data produce imprecise estimates. We can only reduce the influence of randomness; we cannot eliminate it.

Perfection, however, is an unrealistic standard for any evaluation system. From a public-policy perspective, the most important question to answer is whether value-added analysis helps to improve upon the current system's ability to identify the link between a teacher's evaluation and her true performance in the classroom.

If the standard for a new evaluation system is that it has less error than the current system, then value-added clearly passes the test.

Both qualitative and quantitative measures of teacher quality are imprecise. But an important benefit of the quantitative approach is that we can observe the error with which it is measured and make adjustments.

In the case of subjective teacher evaluations, it is impossible for the outside observer to tell how much of a teacher's positive rating is real or fake. We don't know what proportion of it is the result of the principal either misidentifying the teacher's contribution or willfully ignoring her limitations in order to avoid the hassle of justifying a poor rating.

Statistical measures, on the other hand, allow us to measure the potential for error by producing what are known as confidence intervals. The model calculates how much unexplained variation there is in a teacher's average contribution to his students' test scores. The approach then utilizes that calculation to report a range of values of what the teacher's true contribution is likely to be. The model allows us to say, for example, that we are 95 percent confident that the teacher's contribution to student learning is between ten and twenty test score points higher than the contribution of the average teacher in his school. The more precise the model's estimate, the smaller the confidence interval.

When using statistical approaches, then, the precision of the teacher's estimated influence can be quantified and taken directly into consideration. By contrast, we don't know how much of a principal's assessment is based on true performance and how much of it is either incorrectly perceived or compromised by external pressures. In the case of quantitative measures, we can see just how well the statistical model "fits" the data. If the model estimates that a teacher's average contribution to student learning is very poor relative to her colleagues, but her value-added score appears to be measured very imprecisely such that there is a realistic probability that she is doing an acceptable job in the classroom, then administrators can place less weight on the numbers.

Of course, education is not the only sector that evaluates its employees with some meaningful error. No evaluation tool is perfect, and yet employers in the private sector evaluate their employees frequently, both formally and informally. Another potential test for value-added is how well its precision compares with that of statistical tools used outside of public education.

In a report for the Brookings Institution,[25] a team including some of the nation's most prominent education researchers reported that the correlation found between teacher value-added scores from one year to the next is comparable to the year-to-year correlations of factors such as: SAT scores used to evaluate whether students will succeed in college; patient volume and mortality used to rate surgeons and hospitals according to federal guidelines; home sales for realtors; returns on investment funds; productivity of field-service personnel for utility companies; output of sewing machine operators; and batting averages for professional baseball players.

Other sectors know full well that their quantitative ratings of employee quality are imperfect. Yet they continue to use these imperfect measures because they are the best estimates available. Some work hard to improve upon their quantitative measures—for example, the revolution in quantitative analysis of baseball players over the past decade is a direct result of the realization that there is more to a hitter than his batting average. And few if any thoughtful employers use quantitative measures of productivity alone to evaluate their employees. But employers in these sectors are faced with the reality that they need objective measures of their employee's contribution, and they will use imperfect tools for the job.

Perfection isn't an option when evaluating teachers. Deciding whether to use value-added methods to evaluate teachers comes down to determining just how much randomness we are willing to accept, and how to make decisions in the case of difficult calls, where the results of the evaluation are mixed. That decision ultimately depends on whether our intention is to use the evaluation system to protect the interests of existing teachers or to maximize the achievement of their students. This, of course, illustrates the fact that the interests of teachers and their students are not always aligned.

Individual teachers are primarily concerned that their own evaluation score is "fair"—they are justifiably worried about the incidences of "false negatives," whereby effective teachers receive an unsatisfactory rating through little to no real fault of their own. This means that from the teacher's perspective, only extremely precise evaluations are acceptable. From the teacher's perspective, quantitative evaluations will undoubtedly increase the number of false negatives.

False negatives are bad for students as well, but for a different reason: Students could suffer if incorrect evaluations force good teachers to leave the classroom.

But it is in the case of "false positives" that the interests of students and their teachers diverge. Bad teachers benefit from a system that is likely to identify them as adequate despite their performance. Good teachers might find such an evaluation system to be unjust, but they do not find it to be threatening. Things are different from the students' perspective. Students suffer in the form of decreased learning when they are exposed to bad teachers who were never correctly identified and removed.

Of course, the current evaluation system is riddled with false positives. Including value-added assessment into the current evaluation system would surely decrease the number of bad teachers who are incorrectly identified as performing at a satisfactory level.

If we think that student learning rather than teacher protection is the correct focus for schools, then we must ask whether decreasing the number of false positives outweighs the risk of increasing the number of false negatives. The answer is an unqualified yes.

As an example, consider the thought experiment conducted by economists Dan Goldhaber and Michael Hansen. The researchers used a value-added model to calculate teacher contribution to student learning in North Carolina based on their first three years of performance in the classroom, and used these value-added scores to predict student learning in each teacher's fifth year in the classroom. They then considered the likely effects of an extreme policy whereby the public school system simply removed teachers whose value-added score ranked in the bottom quarter and replaced them with teachers who had average effectiveness ratings in their first two years.[26] Their thought experiment took into account that the imprecision of value-added evaluations means that some of the teachers who were let go under this policy would actually have been effective in later years (false negatives), and some who remained in the classroom will turn out to have been duds (false positives). Similarly, some of the teachers brought in to replace the exiting teachers will be more or less effective than their original value-added rating suggested. Their estimates showed that students would have generally benefited from the policy because the benefit of removing truly ineffective teachers would have more than outweighed the cost of losing good teachers.

The lesson of this thought experiment isn't that we should adopt such a Draconian policy. Rather, it illustrates how students are generally better off if we use test scores to help to evaluate teachers, even if some good teachers are harmed by the policy. If our primary focus is student learning, then using value-added evaluations is a step forward.

If students would benefit marginally from a hypothetical policy of removing teachers with low value-added scores indiscriminately, they would benefit even more if value-added analysis were supplemented in such a way that fewer good teachers were incorrectly identified as ineffective. No statistical tool could produce a perfect measure of teacher quality (or anything else for that matter). Because of the serious limitations of the approach, no one who works with these data believes that value-added measures should be used in isolation to evaluate teachers.

Many teachers worry that policy makers and members of the general public are so poorly informed about the limitations of statistical analyses such as value-added that they will use the tool for purposes for which they are not well suited. Can we trust policy makers to use value-added appropriately, or are we simply opening Pandora's box?

Even with limited use there are already some examples of misusing these data that legitimize teachers' concerns. Several well-meaning education reformers have pushed to use value-added assessment in ways for which the models are not well prepared. Recent controversies in Los Angeles and New York City over whether to publicly release each teacher's value-added score are the most glaring examples of the misuse of these analyses. Obviously, policy makers and the public must insist on using these data correctly, otherwise neither students nor teachers will benefit.

If we believe that a teacher's quality is defined by her contribution to student achievement, then it makes no sense to simply throw away information about her effectiveness. But test score analysis cannot entirely replace subjective measures of teacher quality. Principals and other teachers can see context within the school that is masked in models estimated by computers. Value-added analysis, then, can help to point us toward the best and worst teachers, but they cannot do the job on their own.

SUBJECTIVE EVALUATION OF TEACHER EFFECTIVENESS

Probably the most significant limitation of value-added evaluation is that it is a very blunt tool for measuring teacher "quality." We ask more from public school teachers than that they improve math and reading proficiency, but value-added doesn't take any of those other tasks into account. Furthermore, there are many public school teachers whose students don't take standardized tests, such as teachers of subjects not directly related to math and reading proficiency, and teachers of grades that go untested.

The very real limitations of test-score analysis require that statistical measures of teacher quality be supplemented with qualitative measures of effectiveness. School principals are the proper subjective evaluators of teacher quality. Their assessment can be supplemented by those of the better teachers in the school, but the final responsibility of determining whether a teacher is performing up to the school's standard should rest on the school's highest-ranking administrator.

However, we cannot expect principals to truly separate the wheat from the chaff during the evaluation process if the subjective evaluations of tomorrow continue to look like the classroom observations today. Qualitative teacher evaluations should be ongoing throughout the school year and must have teeth.

Rather than once-a-year classroom visits, a robust observation process ought to continue throughout the school year. That's not to say that an administrator should walk into each classroom with a clipboard every day or that teachers should feel that their every word in a classroom could be held against them. But a vibrant school culture is one in which administrators and teachers constantly dialogue about the classroom.

Tellingly, when schools are released from the restrictions of the current system they often pursue models in which teachers are consistently observed, and this procedure often achieves tremendous success. Many of the best charter schools—public schools freed from many regulations and usually collective bargaining agreements with teachers—require teachers to follow an open-door policy. A principal in a traditional public school might observe each teacher in action once or twice a year. Administrators and the most respected teachers at the best charter schools will pop their heads into a classroom once or twice a week—or in some cases, every day. In these schools, everyone is so accustomed to observers that neither the teacher nor the students seem to notice when an outsider has entered the classroom.

Along with providing a richer understanding of what goes on in a teacher's classroom, constant evaluation develops a culture of teamwork and accountability. School administrators and peer teachers are able to discover how a teacher needs to improve and can intervene before a problem gets out of hand.

But far more important than these nuts and bolts is the fact that subjective teacher evaluations have meaning.

Principals need a reason to go through the time-consuming grievance process that is required when their evaluations correctly identify poorly performing teachers. Evaluations that include a subjective component will fail until administrators have the right to fire chronically poor teachers. Ensuring that bad teachers will eventually be dismissed would give principals a strong incentive to take their evaluations seriously.

Some school systems are beginning to experiment with policies that do just that. Colorado, for instance, recently passed a state law that immediately removes tenure protection from a teacher who receives two consecutive unsatisfactory ratings. It is too soon to tell, but theoretically this will provide empowerment and incentive to principals—and consequently result in fewer bad teachers in the classroom.

KEEPING PRINCIPALS IN CHECK

Teachers for their part worry about principals abusing their power. Principals might give poor evaluations based on personality, or to punish those who make waves in the school. Critics point out that before the adoption of job protections such as tenure, many school administrators did in fact arbitrarily remove effective teachers. Poor treatment from administrators was one of the major reasons that teachers fought to unionize in the mid-twentieth century.

Of course, administrators in any employment sector might abuse their power. There is no particular reason to believe that today's public school principals—most of whom worked as classroom teachers at some point in their careers—are any more vindictive or irresponsible than are administrators in the private sector.

But teacher concerns should not be dismissed. Public schools differ in an important way that makes it easier to fathom that principals might actually dismiss effective teachers, unlike administrators in a private sector firm who would resist the removal of productive employees.

We must keep in mind that public schools do not operate in a market environment. An employer in the private sector pays a price for getting rid of effective workers: he earns smaller profits. Public schools, however, don't face the market's wrath. On the contrary, since students are assigned to public schools based on their residential address, the enrollment that drives public school revenues is not altered substantially if the school's performance declines. A principal who wants to get rid of a teacher despite his effectiveness in the classroom need have little concern about the effect her decision will have on the school's bottom line or her own job.

Many education reformers envision a day when school choice forces public schools to confront robust market forces just as a private company does. Even with the recent dramatic expansion of charter schools across the nation, market incentives will not be strong enough to hold subjective evaluations in check. Nor are they likely to be so powerful anytime in the near future.

Subjective evaluations work well in the private sector because they hold stakes for both the observer and the observed. Likewise, an effective evaluation system for public school teachers that hinges on principal discretion must hold stakes for both parties. Absent market forces, the best way that public schools have found to mimic the market's discipline is policies of accountability. A wide body of research shows that public schools respond to the incentives imposed by accountability policies focused on evaluating overall school performance.[27] By tying school performance to the principal's job, we can use accountability to ensure that principals won't act in ways that harm school quality simply because they don't like particular teachers.

To keep evaluations in check, the principal, as the school's leader, should be held accountable for the school's overall performance. Removing those at the helm of consistently failing schools will provide principals with a powerful incentive not to push good teachers out the door: a principal who systematically removes effective teachers will pay the price in the form of lower school achievement, which increases the likelihood that he will be out of a job soon as well.

The quantitative piece of a teacher's evaluation would also help stem the chances that principals would intentionally or unintentionally remove effective teachers. If value-added analysis plays a major role in her evaluation, then a teacher whose students demonstrate learning on standardized assessments will have little to fear from abusive principals. That is, the principal with an ax to grind with a particular teacher must hope that her value-added rating is somehow far lower than her true performance in the classroom. The randomness inherent in the statistical measure of teacher quality could provide this opportunity, but it remains a slight one.

In fact, once it is actually adopted, many teachers may lose their wariness of value-added analysis in their evaluations and become the system's greatest defenders. Objective analysis of teacher quality protects high-performing teachers who are perhaps undervalued in their own schools. For instance, recent research suggests that principals systematically underrate the influence that male and untenured teachers have on student learning improvements. These real contributions to student learning, frequently missed by principals, will become more apparent as the use of test scores increases.[28] An effective teacher who is not particularly well liked or is for some reason undervalued by administration can point to her value-added score as proof that she is helping her students learn.

TOWARD A BETTER EVALUATION SYSTEM

Now this question naturally presents itself: how much should the evaluation system depend on quantitative and qualitative components? States that have recently pursued ways to improve their evaluation systems with test-score analyses have come up with various answers to that question. In each case the debate over what percentage of the evaluation should be based on value-added has been quite heated, with proponents of value-added arguing that quantitative measures should account for at least half of a teacher's rating, and perhaps more than that, while those who are wary of using test scores to evaluate teachers are seeking to minimize its influence.

Of course, attention must be paid to the relative weight given to components of the evaluation system if only because some rule must be established. However, if the introduction of quantitative measures is coupled with improvements to the subjective component as I have described above—most importantly, that principals are held accountable for school performance—then the importance of the weights for accurately measuring teacher quality decreases dramatically.

In the vast majority of cases, value-added assessment is only revealing what everyone in a school already knows to be true: who the best and worst teachers are is an open secret in every public school. If given the proper incentives to do so, principals are generally capable of identifying the best and worst teachers. Value-added analysis simply holds them in check and provides additional information. If everyone's incentives are aligned properly, then the weight given to subjective and objective components of a teacher's evaluation is not particularly important—in the vast majority of cases they will tell us the same thing.

Unfortunately, powerful political forces stand in the way of adopting quantitative analyses even in such a responsible and limited way. Many school systems have not yet developed the technology necessary to conduct value-added analyses for teachers. At this writing, twenty-one states have data systems capable of matching teachers to students.[29] Since under NCLB all states are required to test students in grades three through ten, each state now has the raw data necessary to develop these systems and should move in that direction.

As we discussed in chapter 1, the screens used by the current system are clearly incapable of ensuring that effective teachers instruct all students. Our inability to identify quality before a teacher enters the classroom strongly argues that a better system would identify which teachers are or are not effective and then use that information in such a way that weeds out the ineffective teachers and retains the effective ones.

A well-planned evaluation system that focuses on a teacher's contribution to her students' learning would provide public school systems with tool they need in order to distinguish between their effective and ineffective teachers. But that's only the first step. Improved teacher evaluations will only help to improve teacher quality if the information they provide about teacher effectiveness is actually used to make employment decisions.

4

HOW DO WE COMPENSATE PUBLIC SCHOOL TEACHERS?

How an organization compensates employees goes to the heart of the quality of its workforce. Both individual employers and professions as a whole compete for talented workers by trying to offer the most attractive wage and benefits packages, and how these are structured matters almost as much as their overall value.

Teaching of course is no exception: overall compensation as well as salary structure plays a role in determining who becomes a teacher, how teachers are trained, what subjects they teach, who remains in the classroom, the level of effort they put forth, and which goals they pursue. Unfortunately, in all these ways the current system is ill-designed to attract and retain quality teachers.

It is no secret that public school teachers earn annual salaries that are relatively low compared to other college-educated professionals. There has been some merit in the cries for increased teacher salaries, heard across the nation for at least the past century.

But how those salaries are distributed among teachers is at least as important as their size. The methods used to compensate teachers have changed substantially since the early days of public schooling. Today's teachers are paid according to a single salary structure that takes into account their years of service in the school district and the number of advanced degrees they have earned. It is worth exploring how this system came into place.

Developing an effective system to pay public school teachers is a difficult public policy task. Pure market mechanisms are not a good fit for setting the pay structure of public school teachers. And yet, political governance ensures that teacher salaries remain low and pushes us toward monolith systems that rely on bureaucratic rules rather than the managerial discretion on which firms in the private sector rely.

HISTORICAL TEACHER SALARIES
AND THE MARKET WAGE

The structure of teacher salaries has changed dramatically since the early days of public schooling. Until the beginning of the twentieth century, individual public school teachers negotiated their salaries directly with the school board much the same way that other professionals negotiate their salaries today. Most school systems had in place minimum and maximum salaries for their teachers, with annual standard of living increases. Teachers haggled with the school system for a salary within those boundaries. When deciding what dollar figure was justifiable to keep a certain teacher, the school considered her contribution as well as the salary she would be likely to garner in the outside labor market.[1]

This market system produced very low annual salaries for teachers relative to other workers. Public school teachers earned salaries slightly higher than those made by skilled tradesman, but considerably below those made by professionals in journalism or social work.

Free-market advocates might be tempted to argue that because teachers negotiated their salaries directly with school systems, the outcome must have been indicative of their real worth in the classroom. But while under ideal conditions market-based employment systems should produce wages equivalent to the worker's value, several factors worked against teachers in such negotiations in the past, and likely would do so today if we returned to the market system.

Perhaps the influence cited most often for depressing teacher salaries is the female dominated nature of the profession. The dominance of women began in the later part of the nineteenth century and continues to grow to this day.[2] The male proportion of the teaching workforce dropped from 42.8 percent in 1880 to about a third in 1896,[3] hit 31.3 percent in 1961, and fell to just 20 percent as of 2001 (the last year for which data is reported by the National Center for Education Statistics).

Of course sexism played a direct role in keeping teacher salaries low in the early part of the twentieth century. However, the indirect effect of sexism pulled down teacher salaries as well. Because women were often excluded from other professions and from blue-collar occupations, schools in the early- to mid-twentieth century faced little competition for their employment and thus had the market power necessary to offer low salaries. In addition, the ability to pay female teachers very low salaries depressed the salaries of male teachers for whom women were considered inferior but satisfactory substitutes.[4]

But gender alone didn't keep public school teacher salaries low—teaching was historically held in low social standing, even before its reputation as a job for women emerged. In 1680 the Duke of Sachsen-Meiningen ranked teachers above only day laborers and peasants among his subjects,[5] a sentiment modern teachers might not have trouble believing. Teachers' low historical social standing likely stems from two factors outside their control: first, their service yields an intangible product that is noticed mostly when it is found lacking. And second, in many minds teaching is conflated with child rearing, which while considered important is not regarded as skilled work.

According to economic theory, in a true market system such attitudes about teachers would make little wage difference because employers would be forced to pay salaries equivalent to the teacher's true value, regardless of what the outside world thought. In a market environment, employers want to pay their employees as little as possible, but they are willing to pay wages commensurate with the employee's true dollar worth—in other words, the revenues they bring in to the firm through their productivity. If there are several employers competing for talent, firms will not be able to set low wages because other companies will simply set higher salaries and thus attract the most productive workers.

But teachers are at a disadvantage because the market pressures forcing wages to reflect the true value of a worker's productivity in the private sector are absent in public education. Economic theory suggests that when a business competing in the free market underpays its workers, it is unable to adequately attract, retain, or motivate the workforce it needs and thus is penalized in the form of lower profits. But nonprofit public school systems are immune to these vital market forces. Without the discipline imposed by market pressures, public school administrators face no particular consequences if their teaching talent flees. Lack of market punishment robs teachers of their leverage when negotiating a salary and allows schools to pay wages below the teacher's true value to society.

School systems are insulated from market pressure in that they are publicly governed and funded by taxpayer dollars. They do not compete for their students or resources in a market environment. Many education reformers would like to change that system and introduce some competitive forces within public schools. A sizable portion of my own research agenda focuses on evaluating how public schools respond to competition for student enrollment when it is introduced. However, there is no avoiding the fact that in a taxpayer-funded public school system, operated by the government, the wage value of those who produce student learning—that is, the teachers—must be politically determined. And salaries are rarely if ever efficiently set when they are the direct result of public policy.

Setting teacher wages in the past was complicated by the fact that, at least until very recently, there was no objective way to identify a teacher's independent contribution to her students' learning. An important consequence of this lack of information is that even if society were to accurately price the value of schooling through its policy makers, it would be very difficult to determine which teachers deserved to be paid the most among their peers.

Back when teacher salaries were negotiated directly, without a way to objectively differentiate teacher performance, corrupt practices often ensued. School boards filled teaching positions with friends and family and they paid their preferred teachers higher salaries.[6]

Lacking objective measures of teacher quality, early experiments with so-called "merit pay" failed miserably. These programs, which sought to grant bonuses to teachers who were performing better than their colleagues, date back to at least 1918 when they were relatively widespread in urban environments.[7] Merit-pay programs declined in the middle of the twentieth century and then were revived in the 1960s, before being quickly abandoned again. Teachers complained, likely with cause, that bonuses were allocated unfairly and did not coincide with true effectiveness. The programs bred contention within public schools, an area where success most often occurs when teachers work collaboratively.

The recognition that public school teacher salaries must be set by policy requires a uniform public-policy solution. Around the dawn of the twentieth century, public school teachers and school boards began to adopt a uniform pay system that satisfied political ends and ensured all teachers were paid a reasonable wage. However, that system has several ramifications impeding efforts to improve teacher quality.

THE SINGLE SALARY SCHEDULE

Public schoolteachers no longer negotiate with school systems for their salaries. Unlike other professionals, teachers do not tend to earn performance-based promotions or bonuses during their careers, which lead to higher pay than their less valuable peers. Instead, the vast majority of public school systems use a single salary schedule that is based entirely on the teacher's experience and the number of credentials she has earned.

The single salary schedule has a long history in American public schooling. The push for increased and uniform teacher salaries was spearheaded by the first class of "professional" educators who were coming into public schools during the early twentieth century. Several states began developing teacher-training schools at the close of the Civil War. Graduates of these "Normal Schools" were better positioned to negotiate collectively for fair wages.

Teachers became a political class to be reckoned with at the beginning of the twentieth century, and they used their increased power to negotiate higher wages. The political power leading to single salary schedules predates the influence of modern teachers' unions. Unions existed at this time but were inconsequential, and collective bargaining was barely a glimmer in their eye. Yet, the writing was on the wall that teachers would eventually gain power over the education system. As early as 1936, a quarter century before the first collectively bargained contract between teachers and a school system, Teachers College professor Willard Elsbree foresaw that, "By the virtue of one million votes, a defensible and clearly defined schedule of wants, and a closely knit professional organization, public-school teachers should be more nearly able to 'call the tune' in the years to come than at any time in the history of the profession."[8]

Indeed, teachers were soon able to "call the tune" in salary negotiations. With their new influence, teachers pushed toward a system that would require all teachers to go through a minimal training at a Normal School and to adopt a single salary schedule based on experience.[9] A uniform pay scale would ensure that all teachers would earn a living wage.

A few large cities had established a uniform salary schedule prior to the Civil War. By 1918 about 65 percent of American urban school systems responding to a survey by the National Education Association reported that they had established a salary schedule, though schools outside of the cities continued to negotiate with individual teachers.[10] By 1972, about 95 percent of public school districts had abandoned experiments with merit pay and other forms of differential compensation.[11] Today, single salary schedules remain the norm nationwide.

So the single salary schedule was a common practice among school systems more than a quarter century prior to modern collective bargaining. But molding the salary schedule into its modern form was the task that gave teachers' unions one of their first major victories.

Recognizing the more specific knowledge required to teach older students, early salary schedules offered higher salaries to high school teachers than to those teaching primary grades. Over time, the differences in compensation by grade alienated primary teachers from their colleagues in high schools, and that difference was a major barrier to the movement to unionize public school teachers into a single collective bargaining unit.

In 1968, New York City's teachers' union, the United Federation of Teachers, led by Albert Shanker, convinced the high school teachers to negotiate alongside the primary school teachers. His pitch was for a uniform salary that would not discriminate by grade level taught but rather on the number of credentials earned. The on-average more credentialed high school teachers took the deal and the modern salary schedule was born.

Today, the single salary schedule based on years of experience and credentials is just about universal in public school systems across the nation. Though each school district theoretically determines its salary system through its own collective bargaining procedure, in practice the national reach of the teachers' unions produces a homogeneous salary structure. The numbers differ from place to place, but as a general rule teachers are paid according to two factors: the number of years that they have been in the classroom and the number of credits they have earned toward advanced degrees. There is little to no discretion allowed under these systems.

The factors that don't show up on the single salary schedule are as important as those that do. Nowhere on the salary schedule is there a line item to increase salaries for more-effective teachers. The same salary schedule applies to the school's physics teacher and its physical education teacher. For any teacher, if you know how many years he has been in the classroom and how many advanced degrees he has earned, you have a clear idea of how much money he takes home.

HOW MUCH ARE PUBLIC SCHOOL TEACHERS ACTUALLY PAID?

The image of the underpaid and overworked public school teacher is a cliché in American culture. But an honest consideration of whether we should increase teacher salaries should begin with an understanding of how much they actually earn.

How much do teachers make? According to the National Center for Education Statistics, in 2007–2008 the average base salary for a public school teacher in the United States was just $49,630. On average, public school teachers took home about $53,230 in their school-year and summer earned income salaries.[12] The estimated total income reported by NCES is nearly identical to that reported by the Bureau of Labor Statistics according to its National Occupational Employment and Wage Estimates in 2009.[13] The reported teacher salaries, it should be noted, exclude compensation in the form of health care and retirement benefits, which for public school teachers are generally far more generous than they are for private sector professionals. (We save the discussion of the influence of their benefits on teacher quality for chapter 6.) However, since such benefits are clearly part of an employee's overall compensation, they should be kept in mind when comparing the take-home salaries of public school teachers and other workers.

Teacher salaries in the United States do vary across several dimensions. Teachers in urban school systems take home about $54,880 per year, while the average base salary was about $44,020 for teachers in rural schools.[14] The average teacher with a master's degree earns

$58,460, which is about 24 percent more than the average teacher with only a bachelor's degree. Some teachers earn very low salaries, while other teachers take home six-figure paychecks. The American Enterprise Institute's Frederick Hess estimates that as of 2004 there were at least fifteen thousand to twenty thousand public school teachers in the United States earning more than one hundred thousand dollars a year for their teaching duties.[15]

Private school teachers earn much lower salaries than their public school counterparts. The average total school-year and summer earned income for private school teachers in 2008 was just $39,690—or about three-fourths of the income made by the average public school teacher in the United States. But direct comparisons of public and private school teacher salaries ignore that private school teachers are often motivated to teach by factors other than money. For example, a Catholic school teacher might regard the opportunity to share her religious faith with students as a powerful motivation to do her job even if it pays a very low salary.

Public school teachers are not paupers. According to the Bureau of Labor Statistics, the average public school elementary and secondary teacher (excluding special education) earns an annual salary that is about 22 percent above the mean annual salary in the United States. But teachers do earn relatively low annual salaries compared to other white-collar workers with college degrees. The average employee working in a Life, Physical, and Social Science Occupation (for example, animal scientists, chemists, biological technicians, survey researchers) earns about $65,660, or about a quarter more than the average public school teacher. Those working in Computer and Mathematical Science Occupations on average take home about 44 percent more than the average public school teacher.[16]

Teacher salaries have in fact improved in the past several decades. According to the National Center for Education Statistics, the average public school teacher salary in the United States increased by about 48 percent in real dollars between 1960 and 2009.[17] Nonetheless, public school teacher salaries have not increased enough to keep up with the salaries offered to other college-educated professionals. In 1940, nearly 70 percent of college-educated females and more than half of college-educated males earned less in a year than the average public school teacher. Those figures had dropped to fewer than half of the college-educated females and fewer than 40 percent of college-educated males by 2000.[18]

NONPECUNIARY COMPENSATION

Of course salary is important. But there is more to a job than how much it pays. Our careers play enormous roles in our lives and how we define ourselves. Teaching has several attributes many people find attractive. Such nonpecuniary returns to teaching have an enormous influence on the type of person who becomes a teacher, and will continue to do so whether or not their salaries are increased.

The most obvious attribute offered by the teaching profession is the chance to work with children and make a difference in their lives. Teachers are paid well enough that it is usually not an entirely selfless act to go into the profession. However, the profession will tend to attract those who are not only willing to spend their day with kids but actually prefer that scenario to working in another field. Many great teachers talk about the commitment and love that they feel toward their students and how they are willing to work hard in order to see them succeed. Even the most dedicated teachers wouldn't do such a difficult job for free. But those who have a strong preference for working with students rather than, say, working alone in a cubicle, will be willing to take less pay to do the teaching job than another person who isn't particularly interested in kids.

The structure of the school day is another attractive feature of the teaching profession. Teaching is a very family-friendly job. Teachers of school-aged children can work full-time and still spend time with their own kids when school is not in session. Because their schedules mimic those of students, the time that a teacher spends away from work generally coincides with time that their children are also free from school. Vacations and other holidays coincide with the time that their children are not in school. The benefits of a teacher's schedule is likely an important reason why teaching is a female-dominated profession.

The personal benefits of teaching are quite obvious and clearly important. But teaching in public schools also offers professional benefits that do not show up in an analysis of average wages.

Job security is a highly attractive attribute of teaching in a public school for many people. As we will discuss in a later chapter, after a teacher has been in the classroom for only a few years, she accrues very strong job protection through the tenure process. Once tenured, a public school teacher can essentially not be fired.

The teaching profession even offers safety from layoffs compared to public sector workers: either according to their collective bargaining agreements, or in some cases state law, when teacher layoffs must occur due to fiscal constraints they must be distributed according to seniority. Anyone who has been a teacher for more than a couple years has little (or nothing) to fear from education budget cuts, even when states are bleeding red ink.

There are many other professions in the private sector—and certainly in the public sector—where workers enjoy job protections similar to those granted to public school teachers. These instances are usually found in heavily unionized occupations. Unlike teaching, protected employees tend not to be in careers that require a college degree. Nonetheless, public school teachers earn annual salaries that are competitive with professional public employees such as police officers ($55,180) and firefighters ($47,270). Public school teachers earn substantially higher salaries than those in production occupations (average $33,290 across the sector) where workers tend to be covered by collective bargaining agreements.[19]

In a later chapter we will further discuss the ramifications of layoff provisions on teacher quality. For our current purposes of considering the influence of the size and structure of teacher salaries on teacher quality, what is important to recognize is that the teaching profession is particularly attractive to college-educated individuals who are risk-averse enough that they prefer a guaranteed paycheck to a larger one.

HOURS WORKED BY TEACHERS

Limiting the discussion of public school teacher pay to their annual salaries masks at least one important factor in a teacher's total compensation: public school teachers can work many fewer days and hours than the average professional—and some public school teachers work substantially fewer. The gap between public school teacher salaries and the rest of the working world closes substantially when we consider differences in the work year.

School days typically contain fewer hours than the average work day. Furthermore, like their students, public school teachers are not in the classroom during the summer months and have long breaks and several days off during the school year. The number of working hours required and actually delivered by public school teachers is an important factor in their total compensation and must be considered when comparing their salaries to those of other professionals.

How many hours do public school teachers spend working? People are passionate when answering that question.

It is fair to say that there is wide variation in the hours that individual teachers spend working. There is no reason to doubt the many teachers who report working deep into each night preparing their lesson plans and grading papers. On the other hand, more than a few teachers burst out of school every day as soon as their mandated work time has been completed.

The number of days, hours, and even minutes that a public school teacher is required to work is almost always defined in the collective bargaining agreement with the school district.

Perhaps the strongest evidence that at least some teachers don't exceed the minimum work-hour guidelines is the fact that their unions fight hard against any changes to them. For example, during a recent dispute between teachers and administration in Central Falls, Rhode Island, the school district fired and then eventually rehired all of the teachers in a school. The primary contention was whether or not to amend the collective bargaining agreement in order to lengthen the school day to seven hours. If no teachers paid attention to the minimum-hour requirement, then it would be difficult to imagine why increasing the number would prove to be such an explosive point in contract negotiations.

But, like other professionals, the majority of public school teachers work more than the required number of hours, and many teachers work far more hours than what is mandated of them in their contract. According to a survey conducted by the National Education Association—the nation's largest teachers' union—the average teacher in the United States works for 181 classroom teaching days and 7 nonteaching days, which translated into about 37.4 working weeks. The average teacher is required to work thirty-seven hours a week. However, public school teachers report on the survey that they work an average of fifty hours per workweek on all teaching duties.[20]

The amount of work either required or delivered by the average public school teacher in the United States has changed very little in the past half century. On the same NEA survey conducted in 1961, teachers reported that they were required to work an identical number of hours and days as teachers in 2001. Today's teachers report that they actually work three additional hours a week than did teachers from fifty years before. Meanwhile, teacher workloads appear to have declined since the mid-twentieth century. The median class size in elementary schools dropped from twenty-nine in 1961 to twenty-one in 2001. Class size in secondary schools has remained relatively unchanged during this time period. However, likely due to an increase in the number of planning periods, the total number of students taught by the average secondary school teacher dropped by more than a third from 1966 to 2001.[21]

How a teacher's salary compares to that of other professionals depends on how many hours she works during the school year relative to how much she would work in the private-sector labor market. Table 4.1 translates reported teacher salaries in New Jersey into the estimated annual salary had teachers worked the same number of hours as reported by the average worker in the state.[22]

According to the state's Department of Labor and Workforce Development, the mean teacher salary in New Jersey is about $60,090.

Table 4.1

	Mean	25th Percentile	50th Percentile	75th Percentile
Unadjusted annual salary	$60,090	$47,170	$55,480	$73,260
National compensation survey hours (1,401)	$86,382	$67,809	$79,755	$105,315
Required hours (1,289.25)	$93,870	$73,687	$86,668	$114,443
High-end (1,710)	$70,773	$55,556	$65,343	$86,284

As they do across the nation, teacher salaries vary in New Jersey with teachers at the twenty-fifth percentile earning $47,170 and those at the seventy-fifth percentile earning $73,260.

Teachers who work only the number of hours required in collective bargaining agreements earn average salaries that would be the equivalent of $93,870 for those who work as much as the average New Jersey employee.[23] That's an attractive salary relative to most other professionals.

The table also reports comparative teacher salaries, estimating a workweek of fifty hours on average during the school year. In this case, the average teacher's salary increases to about $65,343 in the rest of the working world, and is $86,284 for the best-paid 75 percent of the state's teachers. Nonetheless, this comparison omits the fact that not only do teachers work far more than the required hours, but countless professionals in other fields work more than the standard forty hours a week. Thus, we can reasonably consider the comparison of teachers' salaries to those of other professionals, assuming a fifty-hour workweek for teachers, to be a very conservative estimate of relative compensation.

ARE TEACHERS OVER- OR UNDERPAID?

So are teachers over- or underpaid? One can make reasonable arguments on either side.

There are many teachers who work harder than much-better-paid workers in other sectors. There are also teachers who take advantage of their strong job protections and bring little effort into the school day. If we paid people according to how much effort they put into their jobs, there would many teachers who could honestly claim to be underpaid, and there would be others receiving higher salaries than they deserved.

We can consider teacher pay in economic terms as well. Some teachers make invaluable contributions to their students' growth as human beings. A teacher who consistently pushes his students to succeed and substantially adds to their proficiency is worth a great deal to society, which depends on highly educated and motivated workers for economic growth. Teachers whose students fall behind their peers and thus become less likely to go to college or become productive members of society aren't adding a great deal to the public purse. If we paid people explicitly according to how much they add to their employers (in this case, the tax-paying public), there would many teachers with a clear gripe that they are terribly underpaid and others who should get a pay cut.

All else equal, we would prefer a system that paid individuals for their contribution to society. But justice is not the policy maker's primary concern. When we consider the public expenditures, the most important question is whether increasing teacher salaries further is likely to contribute to a commensurate increase in student achievement. That is, if increasing teachers' salaries were likely to pay off in the form of substantially higher student achievement, we should increase pay regardless of whether we believe teachers deserve more money.

Expenditures on public education are best thought of as an investment in a nation's future. The quality of educational services provided clearly has value for society as a whole. Public schools provide the educated workforce that propels a nation's economy. At a minimum, policy makers should consider this economic return when deciding how much to invest in public schools and their teachers.

Furthermore, as a wealthy society, we might be willing to invest in a system that produces returns that are not directly seen in GDP growth. For instance, we have the luxury of paying for a school system that enriches its students' lives with instruction in the arts and other pursuits of the mind that make life more appealing but may not be directly related to economic growth. As a society, we should be willing to pay teachers higher salaries if that investment leads to better academic productivity down the line.

CHANGE THE PAY OR CHANGE THE SYSTEM?

The problem with the argument that we should increase teachers' salaries as a form of investment is that there is little reason to believe that salary increases in the current system will lead to substantial improvements in students' academic achievement.

Schools would benefit from a system that pays teachers what they are worth. But the wide variation in teacher quality implies that doing so requires a system for differentiating among the best and worst teachers. The current compensation system doesn't fit the bill. It fails to acknowledge the clear fact that not all teachers are equally effective. What's worse, it only rewards teachers with higher salaries for engaging in behaviors that research tells us are unproductive.

Even more, the pay system does not consider how much effort a teacher puts into the classroom or how much her students learn. It doesn't distinguish between excellent physics and mathematics teachers who are producing tomorrow's scientists and engineers and the poorly performing physical education teacher who adds nothing. Simply increasing salaries in this current system would not address these injustices and would likely have little influence on the quality of people who teach in our classrooms.

Public schools would be better off if great teachers earn high salaries. Jettisoning the current lockstep pay system is the first step toward that important goal.

5

IMPROVING THE COMPENSATION SYSTEM

Andrew is in his sixth year teaching in an urban school system. He struggled in his first year, but reached his stride in year four and is now widely recognized by students, parents, administrators, and other teachers as among the best math teachers in the school. He is consistently the first teacher in his classroom and the last teacher to leave the school. Andrew takes it upon himself to reach out to the parents of students who may fall into the cracks. He makes time for his students during lunch breaks and after school to ensure that everyone is keeping up with the quick pace in his class.

Andrew likes teaching, and he likes that he is good at it. However, there are things about the job that he finds frustrating. He never thought that he'd get rich teaching. But it drives him crazy that Theresa, the school's notoriously bad English teacher who was caught sleeping in her classroom last week, earns substantially more money than he does simply because she is more senior than he is by four years.

For her part, Theresa is happy enough with her current arrangement. She dutifully works the hours mandated of her by the district's collective bargaining agreement. The principal is always trying to get her to help supervise students during her down time, but she quickly reminds him that she is not required to do so according to her contract. The kids don't bother her too much. She has covered the same material in each of the last six years, which isn't particularly exciting, but means that she doesn't have to reinvent her lesson plan. She is also looking forward to the pay bump she gets when she completes her master's degree in about a month. Teaching isn't everything her young, idealistic self thought it would be. But it is worth it to hang on.

We have to wonder about a compensation system that doesn't distinguish between the Andrews and Theresas of the world; there are many of each. The success of a compensation system depends largely on its inherent incentives. Employers want to develop a salary structure that motivates their employees to engage in productive behavior and that can attract and retain desirable talent. The system used to compensate public school teachers described in the previous chapter does not meet either of these important goals.

Among its many failures, the current compensation system does not distinguish between the most- and least-effective teachers, encourages teachers to spend time and resources pursuing advanced degrees irrelevant to student learning, fails to reward effective teachers, and does not discourage ineffective teachers from continuing in the classroom. Making matters worse, the current system's insistence on paying all teachers equally impedes schools from recruiting the talented teachers necessary to instruct students in the subjects, such as math and science, that they need for success in the modern economy.

How much money teachers make matters. Increasing teacher salaries would be the fair thing to do given the difficulty of their task, although as noted simply raising teacher salaries under the current system would have little to no influence on teacher quality. But from the perspective of student proficiency, the problems with teacher compensation have more to do with the way teachers are paid than the amount that the average teacher takes home. The compensation system provides perhaps the best illustration of a consistent problem with the overall employment structure for public school teachers. We profess to know that teachers are important; we understand that teacher quality varies, and yet the system treats all teachers as if they are the same.

The data revolution in education provides the building blocks for a better compensation system. In the previous chapter, we discussed how we can improve the evaluation system using both quantitative and qualitative information in order to better assess teacher effectiveness. The next step is to use that information when determining a teacher's pay. A systematic evaluation system that is tied to real measures of a teacher's influence on her students is the primary tool for developing a compensation system that rewards effective teaching.

INCENTIVES INHERENT IN THE SALARY STRUCTURE

The structure of the salary system determines the incentives that employees consider when they go to work each day. Unfortunately, in education the single salary schedule is completely at odds with what modern research suggests is even reasonable practice. At best, the current system misses an important opportunity to maximize teacher quality by using the salary system to encourage teachers to engage in practices and behaviors that benefit students.

Thoughtful employers can use the salary structure to solve what economists call the "principal-agent" problem. At its core, employers (principals) and employees (agents) tend not to share the same goals. In the private sector, the employer prefers a very high level of production in order to maximize his profits. But such higher earnings come from the hard work of employees who don't personally benefit from putting forth high levels of effort and thus have little incentive to work as hard as they can. The employer can require that individuals put forth at least some minimally set amount of effort in order to keep their jobs, but the situation is complicated by the fact that the employer cannot truly observe the worker's effort level. Lacking the ability to monitor effort, the employer's response is to adopt a pay structure that aligns his employees' incentives with his own. For instance, an employer might adopt some sort of profit-sharing agreement, which would provide the employee with an incentive to increase profits for the firm.

Of course, the above is a simplistic description of a long-standing problem in economics. There are several important issues related to solving the principal-agent problem that are not to be discussed here. But what this framework helps us understand is that the structure of the compensation system almost certainly has implications for an employee's actions. The uniform salary structure based on credentials and experience used by the current public school system has clear incentives imbedded within it. The system's success requires those incentives to be related to the outcome in which society is interested.

Public education is hardly the only sector that pays its workers more for earning additional credentials. Most other professions don't have strict salary schedules like those used in public schools, but it is common for employers to compensate their employees for earning degrees and certifications. Business professionals acquire MBAs because the degree will earn them a promotion at their current job or make them more attractive to other firms. People training to become actuaries routinely receive compensation bumps for each exam that they pass toward earning their FSA designation.

Employers in the private sector pay for credentials because they convey information about the worker's productivity. The hope is that a worker acquires some skills that translate into higher productivity for the firm while he pursues an advanced degree. But it's not even necessary for workers to learn anything of use while working toward the credential for it to be worth something to an employer. The determination to earn a credential can demonstrate a worker's dedication and signal that she is more likely to be highly productive.[1] The private labor market believes that people who have the additional credentials are generally more effective at their jobs. If private sector firms didn't observe that earning a credential was related to productivity, they would have no reason to pay a premium for it.

Similarly, the only logical reason to pay teachers more for earning a master's degree is that it improves or demonstrates effectiveness in the classroom. It would be good practice to encourage teachers to earn advanced degrees if they became better teachers as a result, or if they helped us to identify better teachers.

The single salary schedule provides teachers with a clear incentive to earn advanced degrees, and they have responded to that incentive. In 2007–2008, a teacher with six to ten years of experience increased her base salary about 20 percent by earning a master's degree.[2] With such a considerable return to the additional credential, it should come as no surprise that more than half (52 percent) of all public school teachers in classrooms today have earned a master's degree or higher, compared to only about a quarter of teachers with an advanced degree in 1961.[3] The difference in teacher credentials over the past forty years is even starker if we take into account that in 1961 about 15 percent of public school teachers had not even earned a bachelor's degree (see table 5.1).

The assumption that teachers who earn advanced degrees are more effective than those who do not made perfect sense when the current system was developed. It is reasonable to expect that the pursuit of additional training should both provide the individual with new skills and

Table 5.1

	1961	1971	1981	1991	2001	2006
Highest degree held (%)						
Less than bachelor's	14.6	2.9	0.4	0.6	0.2	1.0
Bachelor's	61.9	69.6	50.1	46.3	43.1	37.2
Master's or specialist degree	23.1	27.1	49.3	52.6	56.0	60.4
Doctorate	0.4	0.4	0.3	0.5	0.8	1.4
Median years of full-time teaching experience	11	8	12	15	14	15

Source: National Center for Education Statistics, Digest of Education Statistics 2010, table 73.

signal their dedication to their profession. Teachers commonly report that they become more effective each year they spend teaching.

Thanks to modern research, however, we no longer need to make such important assumptions blindly. We now have ample evidence that the assumed relationship between credentials, experience, and effectiveness is wrong.

As we discussed in chapter 2, there seems to be no correlation between how we pay teachers and what skills make them effective. Failure to find any relationship between credentials, experience, and teaching effectiveness is perhaps the most consistent finding in educational research.

Such research is clear: earning a master's degree does not make a teacher better. Recall that literally none of the "high quality" studies identified in the literature review by Hanushek and Rivkin found a significant relationship between a teacher possessing a master's degree and student academic achievement.[4]

The implications of these studies are impossible to ignore. The current system rewards teachers for acquiring meaningless degrees, and teachers respond to that incentive by earning meaningless degrees—representing not only a failure to improve education, but a huge sum of lost time and financial resources.

What's even more distressing is that we fail to reward any attribute, behavior, or outcome that is linked to student achievement. Teachers receive no additional compensation for doing a good job. They earn no more money if they work hard into the night grading papers or preparing lesson plans. Effective senior teachers are not compensated for mentoring their struggling junior colleagues. Additional effort in the classroom, or attaining superior results, does nothing for a teacher's bottom line, and conversely, a teacher doesn't find herself earning lower pay if her students consistently struggle.

For many teachers, this systemic failure is unfortunate but inconsequential. Many great teachers work tirelessly to help their students despite the fact that they are not directly compensated for doing so. Teachers might be motivated by the hope of standing out among their peers, or they could just place a high personal value on the success of their students—after all, a big reason that people go into a teaching in the first place is that they love kids and want to help them succeed.

Nonetheless, expecting teachers to put forth their maximum effort level out of the goodness of their heart without any direct financial reward is an odd system indeed. It is also unjust for a system to treat great teachers the same as it treats mediocre ones.

CHANGES IN TEACHER SALARIES AND IN WHO BECOMES A TEACHER

How much we pay teachers has important implications for teacher quality and thus student proficiency. Those whose primary ambition is to get rich don't become teachers, and they never will. But on the margins, higher salaries should tend to make the profession more attractive to those who are weighing the decision whether to become a teacher. Making annual teacher salaries more competitive to those considering other white-collar professions will also help to retain teachers once they have entered the classroom.

There is every reason to suspect that increasing teacher salaries would increase the number of people recruited and retained in the teaching profession. But how we distribute such salary increases has important implications for teacher quality. We don't just want to recruit and retain more teachers. We want to recruit and retain more *excellent* teachers and weed out those who are ineffective. Simply increasing teacher salaries under the current system does very little, if anything, to address the underlying issues.

As discussed in the previous chapter, teacher salaries have increased in real dollars over the past several decades but at a slower pace than those offered in the private sector. This decline in relative earnings has important implications for teacher quality.

The differences in the attractiveness of teaching salaries have been particularly stark for women. In the mid-twentieth century teaching was among the more lucrative options for college-educated females, but that is no longer true today. The decline in the salaries of female teachers relative to other female college graduates is particularly interesting. The exclusion of women from the general labor force through the mid-twentieth century depressed the wages of those women who did work, but the public school system—and subsequently, public school students—benefited from talented women having no other outlet for their abilities.

As employment opportunities opened up for women by the 1970s, public schools needed to compete for talented teachers by increasing salaries. But even with increases, earnings growth for college-educated women outpaced the increase for teachers. No doubt this dynamic drew into the private labor force many women who would have been teachers in years past.

Additional employment opportunities available to women seem to have reduced the qualifications of the women entering the field. For example, SAT scores among teachers have declined, as has the share of graduates of elite colleges entering the field.[5] Research suggests that additional opportunities for women in the labor force are at least in part responsible for those declines.[6]

The single salary schedule has also helped push high-scoring students away from teaching. As intended, the adoption of the standard wage scale led to a compression in teacher salaries; teachers with similar credentials and experience began earning identical salaries, no matter what subjects they taught and to which students. In 1968, the year of Shanker's deal, secondary school teachers earned an average salary that was about 7 percent higher than that of elementary school teachers. As of the 2007–2008 school year, secondary school teachers earned an average of just $218 a year more than elementary teachers.[7]

Any economist would assert that compressing wages in an occupation would push out high-aptitude workers.[8] When top workers are not rewarded with higher wages, they move into other jobs that are willing to pay for their talents.

Changes in relative salaries offered by public education have both pushed and pulled high-aptitude teachers out of the classroom. They have been pushed out of the teaching profession by wage compression at the same time that the private labor market has pulled harder to get talented workers. In fact, some research suggests that wage compression is a bigger culprit in steering top college graduates away from teaching than even expanded work opportunities for women.[9]

Whatever the cause, it is important to keep in mind that the reduction in teacher test scores and the prestige of their credentials in the past several years do not necessarily translate to a reduction in classroom quality. It stands to reason, of course, that it is better to have a highly intelligent teacher than a dunce. But as we learned in chapter 2, factors such as a teacher's SAT score explain very little of the difference in teacher effectiveness. High-aptitude teachers and those who graduated from competitive universities are slightly more productive than other teachers on average. But differences in these measures of aptitude explain very little of the overall difference in the performance of one teacher over another. The quality of credentials held by public school teachers has clearly declined, but highly credentialed teachers are not necessarily highly effective teachers.

Likewise, luring high-achieving women away from education does not necessarily mean that teacher quality will suffer. The skills that make someone an effective teacher are not the same skills that make her a valuable employee in the business world. As we have seen, research shows that very little of what makes one teacher more effective than another can be measured or observed, which includes some factors that are highly prized in the labor market, such as standardized test scores and the quality of college course work.

It is feasible that the sort of person who is attracted to higher wages may not be the sort of person who has the skills that make someone a great teacher. Everyone has some preference for earning money. But some people place a greater weight on monetary gain than do others. Those who prefer the nonpecuniary rewards of teaching—the joy that comes from working with children, the freedom to spend time with one's own family, the rush that comes when someone finally understands what you have been trying to teach them—might also have those intangible skills that translate into teaching effectiveness. That's not to say that we should ask teachers to do their very tough job for chicken feed. But it is worth keeping in mind that teachers—particularly those dedicated to their profession—might be less responsive to salary changes than many other professionals.

The current salary system's failure to differentiate between the most- and least-effective teachers means that changes in compensation influence both effective and ineffective teachers in very similar manners. The differences in the salary and the compression of the salary schedule certainly led many potentially great teachers to choose another profession. But they also discouraged many people who would have been mediocre or poor teachers.

Imagine if we decided upon a policy to increase teacher salaries by 20 percent universally. The promise of higher salaries would compel many more current college students to consider becoming a teacher. That policy would certainly increase the overall supply of potential teachers. Among those who would be likely to give teaching another look would be high-aptitude people able to command better-than-average wages in the private sector.

The problem with uniform salary increases, however, is that they make teaching a more attractive option for everyone, not just to those who could become great teachers. That wouldn't be such an issue if we were able to distinguish between which applicants are likely to be effective teachers and which are not.

Unfortunately, as we saw in a previous chapter, we have no such tools. Nothing that we observe about a teacher before she enters the classroom is an accurate predictor of how well she will perform. Without a reliable way of identifying which applicants will be effective, a large increase in the supply of people who want to become teachers should not be expected to improve teacher quality meaningfully.

Our only hope for improving teacher quality through the compensation system is to target wage increases to those teachers we know are effective.

SALARIES THAT RETAIN THE TEACHERS
WE WANT TO RETAIN

The attrition rate of young teachers is very high. About a third of public school teachers leave the profession after three years. Many of those young teachers leave the profession for the promise of a higher-paying job in the private sector. Thus it stands to reason that one way to increase retention rates is to increase salaries.

Not all attrition is problematic, however. It is a problem when we lose great teachers to the private sector or any other life choice. But it's good when mediocre or bad teachers leave the classroom.

Though there is still much more to learn in this area, some recent research finds that on average, the more effective a teacher is in the classroom, the higher the likelihood that he will remain in the classroom.[10] That's the good news. The bad news is that so many good teachers do leave, and so many bad teachers stick around, that from a policy perspective, the average doesn't tell us much of any interest.

Figure 5.1 comes from a recent paper by Dan Goldhaber, Bethany Gross, and Daniel Player conducted for the National Center for Analysis of Longitudinal Data in Education Research. Teachers to the right of the vertical line have a higher-than-average value-added score, while those to the left of the vertical line make a below-average contribution to student learning. The graph shows that teachers who remain in the classroom have slightly higher average achievement than those who exit the classroom. However, the difference is subtle. There remain many below-average teachers who stay in the classroom and a very high number of above-average teachers who leave the profession.

As a policy matter, we are interested in changing two parts of the relationship shown in the graph. We want many more-effective teachers—those to the right of the line—to choose to stay in the classroom. We would also prefer a policy that leads many of the ineffective teachers—those to the left of the vertical line—to leave for another profession.

Part of the strategy to change teacher quality could include efforts actively to remove lower-performing teachers from the classroom. We will discuss that issue in a later chapter. For now, we focus on keeping more high-performing teachers in the profession. In theory, we can remove ineffective teachers. But we can't force higher-performing teachers to stay.

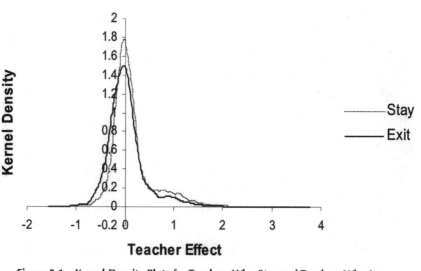

Figure 5.1   Kernel Density Plots for Teachers Who Stay and Teachers Who Leave.
Dan Goldhaber, Betheny Gross, and Daniel Player, "Teacher Career Paths, Teacher Quality, and Persistence in the Classroom: Are Public Schools Keeping Their Best?" *Journal of Public Policy and Management* 30, no. 1 (2010): 57–87. Used by permission.

What policy makers can do is make teaching a more attractive profession for higher-performing teachers than it is for lower-performing teachers. The obvious policy lever to pull is offering higher salaries to the better teachers than we offer to the underperformers. The most important failure of the current system is that it does not target higher salaries to those teachers who are making a difference in their students' lives. That failing is directly related to wage compression caused by the single salary schedule.

Teachers might be less responsive to monetary incentives than other workers. But on the margins, the amount of money that a teacher makes does influence his decision to remain in the classroom. Targeting higher salaries to more effective teachers rather than better-credentialed ones would improve teacher quality by making it more likely that higher performers remain in the classroom and that lower performers leave.

One reason that private firms pay their best employees more money is to provide an incentive for their employees to work as hard as they can toward the company's goals. But even more importantly, employers in the private sector offer wage increases to their employees because they know that they are competing with other firms for their talent. Companies observe which of their workers are effective and which are not, and they seek to retain the more effective workers with higher salaries. Public schools make no effort to differentiate the pay of their most- and least-valuable teachers.

The current compensation system treats all teachers as if their retention were equally desirable. It is not. The wide variation in teacher quality suggests that there are many teachers we really want to keep in the classroom and many others that we'd rather weed out. A salary structure linked in any way to a teacher's effectiveness would help public schools compete to keep the teachers that they want and could help provide an incentive for poorly performing teachers to leave the profession on their own accord.

Let's again consider the influence of a 20 percent increase in teacher salaries under the current system. The higher salaries would provide an additional monetary incentive for an existing teacher to remain in the classroom, and thus we should expect the generous salary increase to reduce teacher attrition. The problem is that the higher salaries are at least as attractive for the low-performing teachers as they are for the high-performing teachers. Sure, there will be several high-performing teachers who might have left for another job, or even to stay at home with their kids, who will think again when offered a higher wage. But there will be many low-performing teachers who will also have been given an incentive to stay in the classroom.

In fact, under some pretty reasonable conditions, it is possible that a universal increase in teacher salaries could actually lead to a decrease in teacher quality. First, if it is the case that lower-performing teachers wouldn't be valued in the outside labor market, then increasing their teaching salary could actually increase the likelihood that they remain in the classroom. Additionally, reducing teacher attrition means reducing the number of positions available to new applicants. Since teacher quality is essentially randomly distributed across applicants, as we have seen, we increase teacher quality on average when new teachers replace low-performing teachers. Reducing the attrition of mediocre teachers then also reduces the number of bad teachers who are replaced with better new teachers.

If we want to increase teacher quality by addressing teacher attrition, it is important that we offer higher wage increases to great teachers than what we offer to lower-performing teachers. If we fail to differentiate the pay of the best and worst teachers, salary increases have no chance of increasing overall teacher quality.

MATH AND SCIENCE TEACHERS

Another concern about salary compression is that it does not allow schools to adjust wages according to subject expertise. A system that pays its gym teachers as much as its physics teachers is problematic both because it fails to correspond with the nation's preferences for student proficiency and also because it ignores labor-market realities.

There is a widespread consensus that skills in the so-called STEM subjects—Science, Technology, Engineering, and Mathematics—are growing in importance every day. By the time that today's elementary school students graduate from high school, proficiency in mathematics and other technological skills will be mandatory for many careers. The American economy needs engineers and scientists in order to remain competitive in the modern technological world.

But even beyond the importance of the subjects, we must acknowledge that the skills required to be a highly effective math or science teacher—particularly in later grades—are almost certainly not the same skills that are required to be a highly effective English literature teacher or general elementary school teacher. Importantly, the technical skills required to be an effective STEM teacher are likely more difficult to acquire than other teaching skills, and they command a different price in the outside labor market. Thus we likely need to offer math and science teachers a higher salary just to get the same quality of teacher in those subjects that we get on average in other, less rigorous subjects. The current system fails to take these clear realities into account.

Public education is competing with the private sector to recruit and retain talent. As we have discussed previously, public schools already offer lower annual salaries to college-educated workers than other white-collar occupations, and they make up some of the difference with other nonpecuniary benefits. But the single salary schedule puts public schools at an enormous disadvantage when competing for individuals with an interest in and talent for teaching math and science. The private sector values individuals with such quantitative skills, and it adjusts wages accordingly.

A recent study by the Center on Reinventing Public Education assessed the compensation for people with technical skills, distinguishing between teachers and nonteachers.[11] The authors found that having a degree in a technical field had no effect on the salary of a public school teacher—that is, those with more technical skills made no more or less than their peers. That's not very surprising, of course, since the single salary schedule does not take such factors into account when determining a teacher's pay. The private sector, however, does distinguish between those with and without technical skills. People who graduate college with a technical major have wages that are on average about 10 percent higher than those who graduate with degrees in other fields.

We know that teaching on average offers lower annual salaries to college-educated workers than other white-collar professions. That is true both for people with and without technical skills. But the important takeaway here is that teaching is a less attractive decision for those who have math and science skills because they are comparing their potential earnings as a teacher—the same earnings as any teacher can expect—to a more competitive wage in the private sector. That is, those with the interest, knowledge, and skills necessary to teach the nation's future engineers and scientists have more competition for their services than do other teachers.

PERFORMANCE PAY

Public school teachers are not equally effective. Nor do all public school teachers have skills of identical value to society. Our current system for compensating public school teachers fails because it does not accommodate for those two basic and undeniable facts.

The call for linking some portion of a teacher's compensation to his performance in the classroom is not new. There have been several experiments with so-called performance pay dating back to the early twentieth century. Each of those early experiments was unsuccessful by any measure and was quickly abandoned. More recent experiments with performance-pay programs are interesting, but have so far produced very mixed results.

It is the data revolution that provides hope that performance pay can be more effective at rewarding high-quality teachers than such programs were in the past. Previous experiments were hampered by a lack of an objective measure of a teacher's contribution to student learning. As we have seen previously, those tools now exist in the form of value-added assessment. We should use an improved teacher-evaluation system in order to target pay increases to those teachers who deserve them.

But even if it operates entirely as anticipated, performance pay is no magic bullet. There are reasons to expect very minimal effects from performance pay in the short term, though it could revolutionize teaching in the long run. Furthermore, there are a series of very serious design issues that we must consider when deciding on how to structure a new teacher compensation system based on rewards.

THE ANTICIPATED EFFECTS OF PERFORMANCE PAY ON TEACHER MOTIVATION

We have seen that paying teachers based on factors unrelated to effectiveness in the classroom reduces teacher quality. Linking a teacher's pay to some measure of performance would help to address many of these issues. However, the nature of teaching and the influence of factors other than pay on teacher quality make performance pay difficult to implement.

The most obvious way that performance pay could influence teacher quality is in creating an incentive to increase student proficiency. Currently, teachers make the same amount of money whether or not their students learn. Effective teaching is a very difficult job that requires not only talent but a great deal of hard work. We provide no external motivation for teachers to put forth any more than a minimal effort in the classroom. By linking a teacher's salary to the performance of her students, a performance-pay program provides a direct incentive for teachers to work to increase their students' achievement by putting forth additional effort.

By aligning teachers' incentives with student development, performance-pay plans should influence effort put forth in the classroom, and thus also increase student achievement. However, there are some reasons to suspect that such additional motivation will have only limited benefit.

The main issue to consider is that the vast majority of teachers already have a high internal motivation to help students. Teachers are college-educated professionals who have chosen to work for relatively low salaries. One important reason that teachers choose to go into the profession is that they want to work to help students succeed.

When thinking of the effects of performance pay, I like to think about a friend of mine who is a public school teacher in the Midwest. She is one of the many great teachers who work tirelessly for her students. In the time that I've known her, I have seen her come home from work exhausted on several occasions, and I've seen her working on projects late on Saturday nights. My friend doesn't work as hard as she does because she expects to get paid more for her trouble. As a public school teacher, her salary does not at all depend on how much she works or how much her students learn. She works as hard as she does because she feels a responsibility to her students to do the best job that she can for them.

How would we expect her to respond to a performance-pay system? It is unjust that she earns the same salary as other teachers in her school who don't work as hard as she does, and more importantly don't make as much of a difference in their students' lives. Increasing her salary would help to correct that injustice. But should we expect that linking her compensation to a measure of her effectiveness—either objective or subjective—would entice her to work harder for her students? Probably not. She is already working near her maximum capacity.

There are many public school teachers like my friend who are already working very hard, even though they receive no financial benefit for doing so. Increasing the pay of such teachers is probably the right thing to do. But it will only marginally increase their effectiveness, if at all.

We would only expect performance pay to substantially increase the effort level of those teachers who are not internally motivated—the Theresas of the example at the beginning of this chapter. Unfortunately, we have many of these teachers in our public schools as well. Some of these teachers got into the profession for the wrong reasons. Others began their careers with the best of intentions but flamed out at some point and are now just holding on until retirement.

Unmotivated teachers might be particularly influenced by external incentives like pay increases, and as a result we should expect performance pay to have an influence on some poor teachers. The anticipated effect, then, is to increase the average level of teacher quality in the system, but by a lesser amount than if all teachers were positively influenced by the policy. Along with increasing average quality, we should also expect performance pay to reduce the variation in teacher quality, since it should push up the achievement of the lowest performers.

There are many teachers who are working diligently for their students despite the fact that their system does not reward them for their efforts. That's a great thing for our children. But a system that relies entirely on the goodwill of its employees to produce results, without compensating them properly, is neither efficient nor just.

THE ANTICIPATED EFFECT OF PERFORMANCE PAY ON TEACHER COMPOSITION

There are many college students sitting in their dorm rooms today considering whether they want to get into teaching or try their hand in the private sector. The salaries offered by those competing choices are an important part of that decision.

More people would consider teaching if they thought that they would be rewarded for being successful, as they would in the private sector. People want an opportunity to work their way up to higher salaries and are willing to take entry-level jobs in the business world because they believe they will be rewarded with higher pay if they do a good job. Public education offers no such opportunity. Someone considering teaching has a very good idea of what she will make over a career, whether or not she works hard and is successful.

Targeting salary increases to effective teachers also has the potential to influence teacher quality through its effect on attrition. By targeting higher pay to those teachers who are making a difference for their students, a performance-pay policy can increase the retention of the teachers we want to keep while simultaneously sending a signal to less effective teachers that we would prefer them not to stick around much longer.

This is where performance pay has the greatest potential to improve teacher quality. By decompressing the wage schedule, performance pay can help to improve the public school system's ability to recruit and retain effective teachers. It can also help us to weed out teachers who are not performing well in the classroom.

However, this is a reform that will show results only in the long term, which is unfortunate given the need for far more immediate improvements.

OBJECTIONS TO PERFORMANCE PAY

As mentioned, there are several hazards that must be taken seriously when considering how to implement performance pay.

A consistent critique of performance pay in the past has been that the teaching profession is so complex and personal that it is not possible accurately to monitor and reward the most effective teachers.[12] That critique certainly held true in the past and would remain true today, if we continue to rely on the current evaluation systems. The lack of an accurate and objectively determined measure of teacher effectiveness was likely an important reason for the failure of previous performance-pay experiments.

Our new ability to use data to measure a teacher's contribution to student learning is a game changer for the efficacy of performance-pay programs. New evaluation systems that incorporate both quantitative and qualitative measures provide a firmer foundation for a performance-pay program than there has ever been in the past.

In addition, one worry is that any quantitative measurement will eventually undermine its own accuracy. Economic theory predicts that when individuals are rewarded for their performance on some quantitative metric, they will find a way to increase their performance on that metric even if it does not also increase real productivity. That is, if we reward teachers for increasing student test scores, they might pursue strategies that increase those scores but do not actually increase the student academic proficiency.

Rather than making students better readers, teachers could focus on pushing test-taking strategies that don't translate into higher student literacy. There have been several anecdotal reports and some compelling research demonstrating that schools and teachers confronted with a high-stakes standardized test manipulate the results, both by so-called "teaching-to-the-test" methods and also by outright changing answers on a student's exam booklet. Attaching a teacher's take-home pay to the results of such exams is certain to exacerbate this effect.

There is no foolproof defense against the possibility that teachers might manipulate the results of student test scores. Egregious cheating can be held to a minimum by strict proctoring procedures and other policing efforts that are costly but likely worth the investment. And qualitative components to all evaluations will be an important supplement and check against teacher manipulation. If we take the threat seriously, we can take actions to minimize test manipulation.

Finally, there are concerns that performance pay will introduce competition into school environments that thrive when they are cooperative. In great schools, teachers see themselves as part of a team. Senior, highly effective teachers can mentor junior teachers and help them to succeed. Teachers can work together and share ideas with each other. If teachers feel like they are competing with each other for pay, the collegial environment found in many great public schools could diminish, and students would suffer for it.

Competition is not necessarily inherent in performance pay, however. Such plans can be structured to reward groups of teachers rather than individuals, and such an arrangement would actually encourage cooperation among teachers. Another alternative is to structure performance pay so that all teachers can earn the same bonuses or salary increases if they meet certain thresholds for performance, and so one teacher's gain is not necessarily another teacher's loss.

Furthermore, it is not entirely clear that encouraging teachers to push themselves in order to be better than their peers would create a toxic environment. We would not want teaching to look like the cutthroat world of investment banking, of course. But there are other professions in which employees compete with each other for bonuses and pay increases without engaging in behavior that is harmful to their organizations.

In addition, the potential for unproductive responses to performance pay is yet another reason that teacher evaluations should contain some subjective component based on principal and other administrator assessments. A teacher who is aiding her colleagues is providing an asset to the school that should be taken into consideration in her evaluation. Teachers who try to make themselves look better by pulling down or at least not helping others are harming their schools, and that should play a role in their evaluation as well. A robust and rich evaluation system for teachers is the cornerstone of an effective performance-pay program.

EXISTING RESEARCH ON MODERN PERFORMANCE-PAY EXPERIMENTS

We expect performance pay to have a limited impact on teacher quality in the short run and potentially larger effects in the longer term. However, keeping that in mind, it is important to consider the relevant recent research examining the effects of modern performance-pay experiments. The results are mixed but tend to suggest that performance pay likely has a limited but positive effect on student proficiency in the short term.

There has been a series of recent studies on the effect of performance-pay programs on student proficiency outside of the United States. International studies of performance-pay programs are useful because the underlying relationships under consideration are no different from those in American schools. We are interested in discovering whether teachers respond to incentives, which is as likely to be true in Ohio as it is in Zimbabwe. However, it is worth keeping in mind that there are important differences between schools in the United States and schools in developing nations that might limit the interpretation of any results for American classrooms.

Karthik Muralidharan and Venkatesh Sundararaman studied the impact of two output-based incentive systems (an individual teacher incentive program and a group-level teacher incentive program) and two input-based resource interventions (one providing an extra-paraprofessional teacher and another providing block grants) in rural India.[13] The individual incentive program awarded bonus payments to teachers for every percentage point of improvement above five percentage points in their students' average test score. The authors found that student test scores increased substantially in schools where teachers were offered bonuses for increasing student achievement. The positive effect on academic achievement was found both on the exam used to provide bonuses and also on other exams that were not linked to the teacher's compensation, providing confidence that the results were not manipulated. Furthermore, they found that output-based programs, where teachers were rewarded for increasing student achievement, had a greater effect than input-based programs, where teachers were rewarded for engaging in certain behaviors likely to be related to achievement.

Paul Glewwe, Nauman Ilias, and Michael Kremer studied the impact of a group incentive intervention that randomly assigned one hundred schools in rural Kenya to either a treatment or a control condition.[14] In this program, teachers competed with each other in a tournament-style competition that paid higher bonuses to teachers whose students made the most academic progress. Students participating in the program had noticeably higher scores on standardized tests than those outside the program. However, students did not achieve similar gains on a standardized test that was not linked to teacher bonuses, suggesting that teachers were indeed "teaching to the test" rather than providing real academic improvement. Indeed, additional analyses conducted by the authors suggested that teachers increased student test scores primarily by improving their test-taking skills, not their overall proficiency.

Economist Victor Lavy evaluated a group incentive program that was implemented in sixty-two Israeli high schools.[15] The bonus scheme was designed as a rank-ordered tournament, with the schools in the top third of performers competing for $1.44 million in awards. The program had a positive effect on the number of credit hours earned, average test scores, and proportion of students taking Israel's matriculation test. Estimates further indicated that the program affected particular groups of students more than others—for instance, students at the low end performed much better than expected on Israel's exit tests.

In another study, Lavy evaluated the influence of a different individual incentive program in Israel that awarded bonuses to high school teachers in grades ten, eleven, and twelve based on their students' performance on national exit tests. The program was structured as a rank-ordered tournament, where teachers competed within their schools to improve student proficiency at higher levels than their peers. He found that the number of exit-exam credits earned by students instructed by a teacher in the incentive program increased by 18 percent in mathematics and 17 percent in English. Furthermore, survey data indicated that teacher attitudes and behaviors improved due to the intervention.

The research findings suggest that performance-pay programs operating worldwide have tended to lead to student academic improvements. Unfortunately, there are fewer experimental studies of performance-pay programs in the United States than there are of those in international programs. Thus, we include a discussion of some evaluations of domestic performance-pay programs that use strong research designs but that do not quite reach the level of an experimental analysis. The research on domestic programs is ongoing but still at a very early stage.

Two US performance-pay programs have been evaluated using the framework of a randomized experiment. A research team led by Vanderbilt's Matthew Springer used an experimental design to study the influence of a program in Nashville, Tennessee, that rewarded middle school teachers when their students made large gains on math assessments.[16] Springer and I also used a randomized experiment to study the influence of a group incentive program in New York City that offered bonuses to schools that made substantial improvements on the city's accountability metric; those bonuses were distributed among teachers in the school by a committee of school employees.[17] In both cases, the programs were found to have no meaningful consequence for student achievement.

There are two nonexperimental studies of performance pay in the United States worthy of consideration. The first is an analysis by economists David Figlio and Lawrence Kenny.[18] The authors analyzed a nationally representative data set and found evidence that schools that had adopted performance-pay programs also had substantially higher student achievement. Their results are suggestive of a positive effect from performance pay, but they could also mean that higher-performing schools are more likely to adopt performance-pay programs than lower-performing schools.

Another recent study of note uses a powerful statistical matching technique in order to study the influence of the Teacher Advancement Program (TAP) on student achievement. TAP, adopted by several schools and districts throughout the United States, evaluates teachers according to a variety of measures—including value-added test score analysis—and rewards them for effectiveness with both bonuses and promotions on a multiple career path. The study compared the performance of students in schools that used TAP to that of students in schools with very similar characteristics but did not participate in the program. The study found that students in TAP schools substantially outperformed students in non-TAP comparison schools.[19]

Though they provide some reason for encouragement, the results from domestic performance-pay programs are less positive than those from international evaluations. What are we to make of these findings? It is possible, of course, that performance pay does not have a similar motivational effect on teachers in the United States as it seems to have on teachers in other nations. However, it is also possible that the domestic performance-pay programs studied thus far are not properly designed.

For instance, consider the structure of New York City's School-Wide Performance Bonus Program (SPBP), which was designed with the cooperation of the city's school system and the local teachers' union. Bonuses were distributed to entire schools if their schools made substantial improvements according to the city's accountability system, which measures student scores on math and reading exams as well as other factors, such as measures of school safety. If a school earned a bonus, it received a lump-sum payment of three thousand dollars per union employee in the school. An in-school committee distributed this money to employees within the schools. The committee could decide to distribute higher bonuses to the most-effective teachers, or to provide equal bonuses to everyone working in the school, including nonteachers. The committee was required to come to a consensus decision; the committee in one school that received bonus money could not decide and was forced to give back the money.

A group incentive program such as New York's provides different incentives for teachers than the tournament-style programs evaluated in several of the international studies. In New York, since the entire school needed to make gains in order to receive the bonus, teachers could only slightly increase their opportunity for additional pay by increasing their efforts. Furthermore, lower-performing teachers could ride free on the hard work of better teachers, since the lack of their contribution only slightly decreased their chances of receiving a bonus. Evidence from international studies, along with some theoretical research, suggests that bonuses targeted to individual teachers and based on a competition to improve student scores might provide a stronger incentive for teachers to improve. However, much more research on US schools is necessary before we can say whether a differently structured performance-pay program would work as hoped.

Furthermore, it is important to keep in mind that studies of existing performance-pay programs—both in the United States and internationally—are only able to evaluate their effect on existing teachers. It is much more difficult to study the effect that performance pay has on the composition of the teacher workforce. As we discussed previously, there is strong theoretical reason to believe that the biggest influence of linking teacher pay to performance could come from its effect on recruiting and retaining more-effective teachers in the classroom.

At this point, it is impossible to determine empirically whether modern performance-pay programs have an influence on the quality of teacher who is recruited and/or retained in the classroom. We would only suspect such a large and systemic effect in the pool of teachers in public schools to occur if there were sizable and clearly permanent changes in the teacher-compensation system. Modern experiments with performance pay have been relatively small in scale, which is appropriate given their unknown effects.

However, some early research findings appear consistent with the idea that, if implemented on a wide scale, performance pay could eventually change teacher compositions in public schools for the better. Survey research by Matthew Springer and his colleagues finds evidence that satisfaction with performance-pay programs is related to the teacher's expectation that he will receive a bonus, indicating that more-effective teachers view the chance to earn higher pay as a benefit. Additionally, the survey evidence suggests that younger teachers are more likely to favor performance-pay programs than are senior teachers, who are more entrenched in the current system.[20]

We have a great deal more to learn about both the short- and long-term effects of performance pay. The research thus far provides reason for some cautious optimism that, when done right, performance pay can lead to student academic improvements.

A SYSTEM THAT MAKES SENSE

Whether or not modern experiments with performance pay pan out, it is abundantly clear that our current system for compensating teachers does not accurately reward our best teachers. There is simply no reasonable justification for a system that pays teachers based exclusively on factors that we know are unrelated to student outcomes.

As is the case for most aspects of the employment relationship between teachers and their schools, the fundamental problem with the current compensation system is that it does not in any way distinguish between our best and worst teachers. We know that teacher quality varies. Our system fails when it does not recognize that basic fact.

6

RETIREMENT BENEFITS

In their vital work evaluating the effects of teacher pensions, economists Robert Costrell and Michael Podgursky present the following hypothetical scenario:

> Ms. Baker is a hypothetical Ohio school teacher, age forty-nine with twenty-four years of service. She's had a good run, but is ready for a change; her heart's not in it anymore, and she wants to go out on a high note. But she has a dilemma regarding her pension. She and her school district have contributed $422,000 to Ohio's pension trust fund (with interest), yet her pension is worth only $315,000. If she hangs on for another six years, the pension picture changes dramatically: her pension will be worth close to $1 million, hundreds of thousands of dollars *more* than the contributions.
>
> Ms. Brooks has the opposite dilemma. She's been teaching in Arkansas since age twenty-five, and at age fifty-three, in light of her exemplary career and continuing enthusiasm, she's just been chosen to be a mentor teacher. The problem is her pension. Every year of additional service *reduces* her pension wealth, despite the fact that she and her district continue to contribute 20 percent of her pay into the fund.

Welcome to the world of teacher pensions.[1]

Obviously salary is not the only form of a teacher's financial compensation; employees also receive—and employers must pay for—benefits in the form of health insurance and retirement plans. We can't understand the failed incentives of public education without considering the size and structure of its benefits system.

Though less obvious than the influence of salaries, the retirement benefits provided to public school teachers have substantial implications for the quality of the American teacher force. Benefits influence both the sort of teachers who are recruited into the classroom as well as the timing of teacher exits.

Of course, teachers require and deserve access to retirement plans that are at least competitive with those available for private sector professionals. The problem is that the way that teacher pensions are structured produces a series of unhelpful and somewhat strange incentives.

THE BASIC STRUCTURE OF TEACHER PENSIONS

Most professionals in the private sector are enrolled in what are known as defined contribution (DC) retirement plans, in which employees and employers jointly contribute to a 401(k) or similar investment device. As the employee, you own the account, so if you leave your job, you take it with you into your new position. You also control the account's investments. At the time of retirement, you will be entitled to collect (after taxes) the full account, which includes the cumulative contributions made by yourself and your employer(s), plus the return and interest accrued over the life of the account.

Teacher retirement plans look nothing like this. As public sector employees, public school teachers are almost universally enrolled in what are known as defined benefit (DB) pension plans, similar to those that once dominated the private sector but have now been all but abandoned there.

As is the case in the private sector, both the teacher and her employer contribute regularly toward the teacher's retirement. But as the name suggests, what distinguishes a DB plan is that the teacher is promised a certain known level of income at the time of her retirement; this amount depends upon the number of years of service.

After a teacher vests into the system—usually after five or ten years—she becomes eligible to receive a full pension that is determined as a function of the number of service years in the school system and her annual salary at the time of retirement.[2]

A teacher's pension wealth is not determined primarily by contributions; the value of her pension does not accrue smoothly over time.

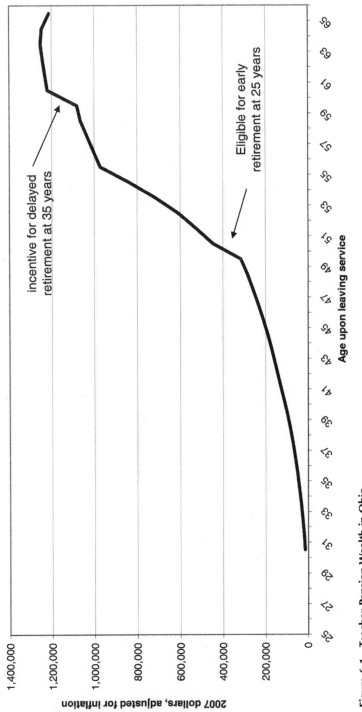

Figure 6.1 Teacher Pension Wealth in Ohio.
Robert Costrell and Michael Podgursky, "Peaks, Cliffs, & Valleys," *Education Next* Winter (2008). Used by permission.

That's because in particular years certain eligibility criteria are met that entitle teachers to a much higher lump-sum amount in their pension.

Figure 6.1, reproduced from the Costrell and Podgursky article, illustrates the accrual of a teacher's pension wealth according to the DB plan in Ohio described in the hypothetical example at the beginning of this chapter. The teacher's pension wealth—that is, the actuarially determined total amount of money that the teacher would likely receive in her lifetime from pension payments if she retired in a particular year—is very low for the first twenty-four years of service. Then, suddenly at age fifty, the teacher becomes eligible for a much larger number of pension dollars. Both the teacher's and the school system's contributions to the teacher's retirement is the same in each year. What changes in year twenty-five is the teacher's status in the pension program.

Compare the strange shape of a teacher's retirement benefit to that of a DC plan for private sector workers. You and your employer contribute a portion of your salary into a 401(k), which allows you to allocate that money to investments that may appreciate over time. If contributions and investment returns remain about the same over time, what your retirement plan is worth to you also accrues at a steady pace. Under a conventional DC plan found in the private sector, there is no magic number of years of service at which point the employee becomes eligible for a big lump-sum increase in retirement wealth.

PAYING FOR PENSIONS

From the taxpayer's perspective, probably the most pressing fact to know about public school teacher pensions is that they are bankrupting you. The Pew Research Center projects that state pension plans will be around $2.7 trillion short of their obligations in the upcoming decades.[3] Similarly dire predictions exist for a variety of public and private institutions.

These shortfalls are the result of two factors: the generosity of the pension plans and the fact that many states neglected their obligations to fund the pension system every year. Those two poor fiscal choices have played a large role in pushing some states to the cusp of insolvency.

Teacher pensions tend to be far more generous than those offered in the private sector. Individual teachers' contributions to their retirement plans are usually far below those of private sector employees. These relatively small contributions to their retirement accounts are likely to result in teachers collecting substantially more in retirement than they contributed while they were working.

Another part of the pension fiscal crisis is that many states pushed off paying their share of the funding obligation. Private sector employers contribute real dollars to their employees' account each year. State governments don't do that. Instead, rather than contributing as they go, states have frequently kept the money and spent it on something else. Thus, they owe retirees money that they have not been saving, and the bill is coming due.

Defenders of the current pension systems are quick to point out that there is nothing inherent in them that would produce financial instability. Policy makers didn't have to agree to such generous terms. It was lawmakers, not teachers, who chose not to keep up with their contributions in order to fully fund the plans. These defenders are technically right.

Policy makers aren't forced into their bad fiscal decisions. But the structure of the DB system makes bad behavior simply irresistible for shortsighted politicians. Public sector employees fight hard for better benefits in several ways, including by working to elect sympathetic policy makers willing to provide generous pensions. As importantly, politicians have an incentive to borrow money from tomorrow's pension obligations in order to fund politically popular programs today. That is, pensions allow current politicians to offer attractive benefits to their political supporters using money that is earmarked for the future without affecting current spending or raising taxes today. Unfortunately the political calculus leads to obvious results: eventually the financial promises made will outstrip the ability to pay for them in the future.[4]

PENSIONS AND TEACHER QUALITY

The problems with pension funding are dramatic and are gaining immediacy, but they do not in themselves directly threaten teacher quality. The issues with teacher pensions go beyond unfunded taxpayer obligations.

Even if DB systems were financially sustainable, their design has substantial implications for the sort of teacher who is recruited and retained in the system.

It seems odd that an attractive benefits system could detract from teacher quality. If benefits are just another form of compensation, why would it be troubling for public school systems to offer teachers a generous deal? In fact, it would seem that the opposite should be true: the attractiveness of the benefits system could help to mitigate the influence of relatively low annual teacher salaries and thus help efforts to recruit effective teachers.

However, as is the case with salaries, the structure of the benefits system is as important as the size of the benefits granted to teachers.

SHOULD I STAY OR SHOULD I GO?

The lumpiness of the pension wealth accrual sets some clear but seemingly arbitrary points in a teacher's career as to when she should retire. It also has important financial consequences for those teachers who move out of the school district or the state, or for those who decide to leave for another profession. Inasmuch as they determine who is teaching in our public schools in any given year, each of these factors has important implications for teacher quality.

Teacher attrition is very high in the first three to five years, and then drops like a stone after that. Unsurprisingly, just about no one retires in the few years before they become eligible for the substantial pension increase—they would be crazy to do so! As the hypothetical situation discussed at the beginning of this chapter illustrates, for teachers with more than twenty years of experience, another year or two in the system can mean hundreds of thousands more dollars in retirement income over their lifetime. Teachers are well aware of these pension bumps and plan their exits accordingly.

There are many teachers who fit the descriptions of one of the two teachers in the example at the beginning of this chapter. Some people burn out of teaching before they hit that magic retirement number and are compelled to stick around longer than either they or the school system would like. There are other fantastic teachers who are in no mood to retire in their mid-fifties, which is when the jump in retirement income usually arrives, but are actually punished by the system for doing so.

But it is not only teachers near the threshold for the pension increase who are affected by the structure of the current system. Perhaps more importantly, the current system is structured so that it reallocates money from certain teachers to others. It rewards teachers who remain in the same school system for their entire professional careers—twenty-five to thirty years—and punishes those who change school systems or leave the profession.

Timothy is in his fourth year working as an accountant in a large company in Columbus, Ohio. Like most other professionals, he is enrolled in a conventional 401(k) program. Each month he sees the amount in his retirement account grow a little more due to his contribution and the contribution of his employer, along with returns on his investment portfolio. Timothy's wife, Sara, is a teacher in a local public elementary school. She's enrolled in the state's DB pension program.

The married couple has decided that they want to move closer to their extended family in North Carolina, and both have found new jobs in their fields. Timothy is rolling over his 401(k) portfolio and will keep every dime that both he and his employer have contributed, as well as the small investment return it has already achieved. Sara, on the other hand, has not yet vested even minimally into her retirement plan. She brings over none of her retirement contributions and must start over. The money that she and the school system put into her retirement account will now help pay for the retirement of other teachers who retire in that district.

Sara loses all of her retirement account because she has not yet vested into the program. But the lumpy accrual of the pension contribution harms even vested employees who leave the system. The structure of the pension system serves as a hefty tax on teacher mobility. Costrell and Podgursky estimate that teachers who split a thirty-year career across two state pension plans will retire with about half of the net pension wealth of a teacher who spent the same thirty years teaching under a single state plan.[5]

For those who are sure that they want to remain teachers for twenty-five or thirty years in the same public school system, this non-portability is highly attractive. Teachers who stay put reap the benefits of teachers who forfeit part or all of their pension contributions.

From the perspective of teacher quality, what matters is that both good and bad teachers have the incentive to hold on to their jobs until they maximize their retirement benefits.

Think about a teacher who burns out and loses her passion for teaching in her fifteenth year. Her performance in the classroom suffers, and her students are unhappy and underperforming. Burning out doesn't make her a bad person—many people need a change of jobs or even careers after fifteen years of doing the same thing, and a teacher's job is difficult enough that many people likely can't succeed at it for thirty straight years. The teacher might be unhappy enough doing her job that she actually wants to leave the classroom. But the pension system keeps her there. Why? Because if the teacher leaves the system she does so with a miniscule retirement account because she has not reached that magic number of service years. If that teacher had been contributing into a 401(k) plan instead of waiting for her DB system to kick in, she could leave the classroom without harming her retirement portfolio.

Nonportable pension systems are extremely unattractive to young professionals who are unsure whether teaching is the right job for them. Furthermore, the current pension system is not very appealing for anyone planning to be a lifelong teacher but who thinks that they might want to move to another state sometime in the next twenty to thirty years. There are many potentially very effective teachers who fit both of these descriptions.

Consider a talented college student sitting in her dorm room right now thinking about whether she wants to try her hand at teaching. Perhaps she is considering accepting an offer to work in a low-performing public school as a Teach for America corps member. She might find the idea of a generous retirement system to be an attractive benefit of teaching. But she will only acquire the full value of that benefit if she decides to remain a teacher for twenty-five years and doesn't move to another state during that time. If within five years she decides teaching is not for her, then she will lose all of her retirement money.

We want talented young people to try teaching if they are so inspired. Many people who walk into the classroom will fall in love with it and will be great teachers for years and years to come. The current pension system is an impediment to those who otherwise might give teaching a try.

It is unsurprising, then, that younger teachers are far more likely to support movement toward a DC retirement system than are long-time teachers, whom the system benefits already. In Washington State, 48.6 percent of teachers surveyed said that if they had an additional 10 percent of earnings to invest into retirement they would prefer to use a DC plan, while only 25.9 percent said that they would prefer the money be invested in a DB plan. (The remaining teachers were unsure what they preferred.) However, support for DC plans differed substantially by experience level. Teachers with nine to fifteen years of experience were 51 percent less likely to support a DC retirement plan than were teachers with fewer than three years of experience; teachers with fifteen or more years in the classroom were more than 70 percent less likely to prefer a DC plan.[6]

BACK-LOADED COMPENSATION

An additional problem with the structure of public school teacher benefits is simply their size: They are too large.

Of course, teachers should receive adequate benefits to provide for their health and retirement. As professionals, teachers should earn benefits that are on par with the private sector. But benefit packages can become so generous that they reallocate too many dollars from current salaries to the future. Public school teacher benefits reached that point long ago.

States spend a fixed amount of money on a teacher's total compensation, and that total spending figure is allocated across the teacher's take-home pay and her benefits package. The relationship between teachers' salaries and their benefits is strikingly imbalanced. For instance, Costrell calculates that in Milwaukee, Wisconsin, the school district contributes an additional 22.6 cents for each dollar of a teacher's salary in order to pay for pensions and Social Security; the corresponding average in the private sector is about 13.4 cents per dollar of salary.[7] Milwaukee isn't alone. According to Joel Klein, former chancellor of New York City's public schools, the city's average annual per-teacher salary is about $71,000, and the city's contribution to the teacher's pension is about $23,000.[8]

What if some of the dollars currently allocated to teacher pensions were instead redistributed to teacher salaries? Consider the New York

City example. According to the above figures, if the city mirrored the private sector's annual contribution to salaries and pensions, it could offer an annual salary above $80,000 without increasing its total obligation to the teacher's compensation. Klein wonders how recruitment efforts would fare if rather than paying teachers a $45,000 starting salary with minimal increases in the early years, the city reallocated the pension contribution to salaries and thus started teachers at around $55,000 with large increases in the first several years of teaching.[9]

How many current and potential teachers would prefer to have some of their pension money today rather than in the distant future? What would be the likely opinion of a talented college student sitting in her dorm room right now considering whether she wants to give teaching a try but is scared off by the relatively low annual salary?

This thought experiment can certainly extend too far. We wouldn't want to reallocate all of a teacher's compensation to take-home salaries for the same reasons that we wouldn't want to remove retirement plans in the private sector. But there is no reason to believe that teachers are such irresponsible people that their total compensation needs to be so heavily weighted toward their retirement in order to ensure they have enough on which to live.

WHO BEARS THE INVESTMENT RISK?

From the employee's perspective, the most attractive feature of a DB-style retirement plan is that it produces a guaranteed return. Under DC plans the employee bears the investment risk: if your portfolio of investments does well, you retire with more money. But if they perform poorly then you retire with less. DB plans guarantee teachers a known income in the future. Under such plans, it is the taxpayer, not the teacher, who is on the hook.

It is possible that teachers are more risk-averse than are other professionals. Perhaps as a group they are willing to trade flexibility and the potential for an even larger return for the guarantee that they will receive a certain pension amount.

We can improve upon the incentives of the current system while still guaranteeing teachers a rate of return on their investment portfolios. Over the past two decades, many large corporations that formerly used DB programs have switched to what are known as Cash Balance plans.

Similar to a 401(k)-style system, a Cash Balance plan closely ties an employee's retirement benefit to contributions. The difference is that these plans guarantee a certain return on the employee's contribution—usually at the rate of a risk-free bond.[10] Restoring the link between contributions and pension wealth would eliminate the arbitrary jumps in pension wealth characteristic of the current system, while the guaranteed return would eliminate any investment risk on the employee's end.

Whatever teacher pension reform includes, it must not embody the perverse incentives and disincentives of the current system, and it must completely reject the unsustainable cost structure the current system has locked us into. This is critical to recruiting talented young people into the field, and allowing them the unfettered job mobility their peers enjoy.

7

WHO SHOULD TEACH?

Jane was accepted to the college of her dreams due to her hard work (a high GPA and lots of AP classes), stellar SAT scores, and a magnetic personality that came through in her interviews. Her university experience unfolded much as she hoped—she made lots of new friends, became editor of the school newspaper, acquired a long list of professors eager to recommend her for any job she chooses to pursue, and graduated near the top of her very competitive class.

Since she was a little girl she has dreamed of becoming an engineer and she was excited when she was offered a position in a mid-sized firm. But as graduation approaches she is getting cold feet. She is thankful for all the advantages she has had in life and feels compelled to give something back. She likes the challenges that her new firm has promised and likes the idea of earning a corporate salary, but to Jane money isn't everything.

Sometimes Jane envies her roommate, Alice, who after graduation will start her first year teaching in a public school. Throughout their four years living together, Jane always considered Alice's education school course work to be less than rigorous, and that didn't appeal to her competitive nature. But Jane finds the idea of helping kids very appealing, especially if she can work with disadvantaged students. She is passionate about mathematics and wants to instill that passion into young people who are likely to believe math plays no meaningful role in their lives.

After some careful thought, Jane decides that she's willing to give teaching a try. At worst, she will work helping kids for a few years, and if she doesn't like it she will surely find another engineering job without too much difficulty. Or, perhaps she will love it and decide to make it her career. She meets with a principal in a local middle school who would love to make her an offer.

There's only one problem: According to the public school system, Jane isn't qualified to teach mathematics. Her mastery of the subject, strong interpersonal skills, obvious talent, and her desire do not compensate for her lack of a teaching degree. She is simply not allowed a chance unless she goes back and earns a certification. Disappointed, Jane takes the job at the engineering firm and eventually makes partner.

Alice, on the other hand, enters teaching as planned. She treads water in her first couple of years and, as a matter of course, receives tenure after year three. But after six years in the classroom, Alice begins to slip. She is routinely unprepared for class. She frequently fills up class time by showing popular videos. Her students like the class, but they are not challenged by it. Every year Alice's principal knows that her students will have made the smallest increase on the state's standardized math exam in the school, and that more of her students will find themselves in a remedial math program the next year than the students of any other teacher.

Her principal would prefer that Alice moved to another school, or even better, out of teaching entirely. But if he tried to fire her she would file a grievance, and he would be forced to go through a legalistic process for which he has no time or resources and stands little chance of success. Each year, he sends students into Alice's class knowing full well that they are unlikely to learn very much.

A manager's most fundamental responsibility is to recruit and retain effective employees. As we discussed in the previous chapter, the structure and size of salaries is an important tool used for this task. But even more important is ensuring that schools become open to qualified candidates of different backgrounds. Equally critical is the ability to remove poorly performing teachers from the classroom.

Once someone passes through the series of hurdles in place to become a teacher, we basically assume that all teachers are equally effective. Very early in their careers teachers are granted job protections that secure their positions not only from layoffs due to budget cuts, but also from poor classroom performance.

This would only be rational if most teachers were essentially equal. Of course, this assumption simply does not hold. Teachers are not all the same. The screens used to ensure minimal teacher quality are ineffective.

And years of experience—the characteristic most prized in the current system—tell us next to nothing about the teacher's effectiveness in the classroom.

We need to turn the current system on its head. Rather than making it difficult to become a teacher and then essentially leaving those who happen to qualify to their own devices, we should open the floodgates and allow many more people into the profession, supporting them in their early years, and then working hard to distinguish between those we want to keep in the classroom and those who aren't cutting it.

REQUIRED TEACHER TRAINING

Before someone can become a public school teacher he or she must earn a license, usually by graduating from a college of education. It seems like a simple enough requirement: no one should teach in a public school before he or she has been exposed to the pedagogical training necessary for success in the classroom. However reasonable it seems on its face, that requirement has failed to keep bad teachers out of the schoolhouse door, and it unnecessarily eliminates many potentially excellent candidates.

Teaching is hardly the only profession that requires a degree or certification. Lawyers must pass the bar; doctors must complete medical school; accountants and even hairstylists must be licensed; the list goes on and on. It stands to reason that teachers who have studied their craft in an education college will be better prepared to take on students than others.

But the reality is that what teachers are learning in those colleges doesn't translate into effective instruction in the classroom. In fact, few seem to believe that teachers leave their college programs more prepared to teach than they would have been without the experience. Why, then, should we continue to insist that people check this unnecessary box before they enter a classroom?

Formal teacher training in the United States began in so-called Normal Schools that grew along with the common school movement of the mid-nineteenth century. These institutions of professional training were meant to develop a class of highly qualified educator. But these schools had to weigh the ideal of well-prepared educators against the real need for warm bodies to fill the nation's expanding number of class-rooms. Normal Schools responded by loosening admissions and gradu-ation criteria. As the need for teachers increased over the next century, teacher education morphed first into the framework of regional colleges and then into the modern university setting, which was better able to provide instruction to large numbers of people.[1]

The relationship between universities and their colleges of edu-cation has always been uneasy, requiring trade-offs between the two. By housing teacher-preparation programs, universities increase their enrollments considerably, receiving full tuition from relatively low-cost students. Education colleges are cash cows for universities. But by incor-porating colleges of education, universities generally have had to reduce their admissions standards in order to fill the programs to capacity.

For its part, the education profession improves its prestige by align-ing with universities. Teaching has always received less honor than it deserves, and making teacher training a part of the university system (rather than its own stand-alone certification program) helps improve that standing. Providing training in the university also allows teacher colleges to recruit students who are interested in teaching but who seek a liberal arts education as well.

This too spawns a trade-off—with educational training limited to a series of courses within a larger academic program, substantially less time is available for pedagogical practice, in-classroom training, and other skills.[2]

There are some good and bad reasons for the makeup of the mod-ern education college. Regardless, it is difficult to find anyone who is satisfied with the quality of its product.

The Education Schools Project recently surveyed groups of public school principals as well as deans, faculty, and alumni from colleges of edu-cation to find out how well they think education school graduates are pre-pared across eleven competencies. Only 40 percent of principals reported that their schools prepared teachers very well or moderately well on each of the competencies. Deans, faculty, and graduates were happier with the product than were principals, but their responses hardly showed a resound-ing vote of confidence: an average of 56 percent of deans, 54 percent of faculty, and 58 percent of alumni reported that education colleges prepared their teachers well across all competencies.[3]

Why are education colleges so ineffective at preparing young teachers for the classroom? One factor is the inclusion of academic research within education departments. While we should welcome serious academic research, this has had the unfortunate effect of reducing the amount of actual classroom training. Arthur Levin, former president of Columbia University's Teachers College, has argued, "In their effort to obtain acceptance, teacher education programs attenuated their ties with P–12 schools and the people who work in them. They attempted to remake themselves in the image of arts and sciences colleges, emphasizing theory over practice and education of academicians over practitioners."[4]

If they are to remain attached to universities, it is appropriate for education schools to conduct high-quality academic research. However, if we take seriously the notion that teaching skills can be taught, hands-on teacher training ought to play a central role in education schools.

KEEPING GOOD CANDIDATES OUT OF THE CLASSROOM

Teacher education doesn't seem to be making teachers better. But there is no reason to believe that it is making them worse. Prospective teachers aren't learning techniques that are actually harmful for student learning. Requiring teachers to graduate from an education college, then, seems at worst to be a harmless requirement.

The problem with requiring teachers to acquire needless training in education colleges is that it substantially reduces the pool of people who are willing to give teaching a try. Many potentially great teachers are kept out of the classroom because they did not acquire training that would not have improved their effectiveness anyway.

The history of teacher education is that of weighing the need to train effective teachers against the need to produce ever more teachers. As a result, education colleges try to ensure that all teachers meet a minimal standard, but that standard gets reduced over time in order to continually increase the number of graduates. The quality of training provided in education colleges generally appears to have declined to such a degree that it is essentially meaningless as an academic subject.

There is nothing inherently wrong with setting up barriers to enter a particular profession; setting a high bar can maximize the chance that the people who enter into a given profession have strong cognitive ability, self-motivation, and organizational skills. This works in law, medicine, architecture, and other rigorous fields. Even if prospective teachers didn't learn anything of use at all during their time in an education school, the requirement would be worthwhile if the people who make it through are better teachers than those who don't—or who are too discouraged even to try.

The training requirement could have such a positive effect on the teaching profession, if a high bar were being set. Requiring teachers to graduate from an education college does mean that the prospective teacher is someone who is confident that she wants to make education a long-term career. Thus the training requirement will tend to remove from the pool of potential teachers those who might have an interest in the profession but are not sure that they want to make it their life's work.

Whether conventionally trained teachers are more effective than others is an empirical question. Because of the growth of alternative teacher-certification programs over the past two decades, we have data demonstrating that graduation with an education degree has no effect on whether a teacher will be successful. In fact, those teachers who enter public schools without having set foot inside an education college are at least as effective as their conventionally trained colleagues.

ALTERNATIVE CERTIFICATION

The growing need for high-quality teachers has produced a wide-scale experiment with alternative certification programs. The idea of these programs is to recruit people who did not graduate from an education college. These programs vary in the type of person they recruit. Some programs recruit professionals seeking a career change, another recruits soldiers, and the best-known program, Teach for America, recruits bright recent college graduates.

Jane from our earlier example would be a candidate to enter the classroom through Teach for America (TFA), which is by far the largest alternative certification program in the United States. The idea for TFA famously came from its founder's undergraduate thesis at Princeton. The organization is modeled on the Peace Corps, recruiting bright graduates from competitive universities to teach for at least two years in impoverished urban public schools. Founder Wendy Kopp reports her thesis adviser told her that her idea was "quite evidently deranged."[5] Yet after two decades in operation, TFA has placed more than twenty thousand teachers into needy public schools.[6] In 2010 alone, TFA placed more than 4,500 teachers—very few of them education-school graduates.[7]

TFA has a presence on college campuses across the nation—not just in the Ivy League—where it recruits successful students with an interest and passion for reforming K–12 education. Those who make the cut after a rigorous screening process are enrolled in an intensive six-week summer course on how to be an effective teacher. They are then placed at the head of classrooms in public schools nationwide that are serving difficult-to-educate students, for a minimum two-year commitment. TFA provides ongoing pedagogical training and guidance to its members.

TFA's recruiting success has shown that there are many very talented people eager to give teaching a try. In 2010, 47,000 upcoming college graduates applied for a spot in TFA. Among that group were 18 percent of Harvard's senior class and 40 percent of Harvard's African American seniors.[8]

How do TFA teachers perform in the classroom? The honest answer is that some of them turn out to be fantastic teachers, some of them turn out to pretty bad, and most of them are a little better than the average. That is, they are not so different from teachers who enter teaching through the conventional route.

There have been many empirical studies evaluating the effectiveness of TFA teachers over the past several years. So many, in fact, that the research findings appear muddied. Some studies find that TFA teachers are performing extraordinarily well in the classroom, while some others find that they do not perform as well as conventionally credentialed or more experienced teachers. However, not all empirical research is of the same quality. An honest look at the most credible research to date suggests that TFA teachers on average are no worse, and likely a little more effective, than conventionally trained public school teachers.

To date, only a single study uses a randomized experimental design—conventionally known as the "gold standard" of social science research—to compare the performance of TFA teachers to those of conventionally trained teachers. The study, conducted by researchers at Mathematica Policy Research, involved randomly assigning students into classrooms of TFA or non-TFA teachers, thus ensuring a fair comparison. The authors then compared teacher performance within the same schools and within the same grades. The study took place in six major regions of the country—Baltimore, Chicago, Los Angeles, Houston, New Orleans, and the Mississippi Delta—across seventeen schools in one hundred classrooms. The authors found that students of TFA teachers did slightly better in math and no better or worse in reading, compared to students who were assigned to other teachers in the school. The magnitude of the improvements made by students assigned to TFA teachers in math increased when they were compared to students assigned to other novice teachers.[9]

The strength of its random assignment design makes the Mathematica analysis superior to other TFA studies. However, other high-quality research confirms that study's findings, while still others indicate that TFA teachers actually outperform other teachers.[10] There are some studies, of lower-quality design, that find that TFA teachers perform less well on average than their colleagues, though even in these cases the differences in teacher quality are very small.[11]

The cumulative findings can be interpreted that the average TFA teacher is no worse, and probably slightly better, than the average traditional teacher of any experience level. Moreover, TFA teachers are almost surely better than other new teachers with freshly minted degrees from education colleges. TFA teachers are not uniformly superstars: they are just about, but not quite as likely to be, as ineffective in the classroom as any other teacher.

Some might interpret these findings as evidence that TFA has been unsuccessful at improving teacher quality. Perhaps. But an equally valid way of interpreting the research is that conventionally trained teachers are at best no more effective than kids who were exposed to a six-week summer course (with additional mentoring throughout the year). "What we've learned," according to Wendy Kopp, "is that there are limits to what any pre-service training can do."[12]

The training provided in education colleges appears to have no bearing on teacher quality. But the training requirement would still make sense if it bore a positive influence on who became a teacher. Are students who graduate with an education degree more dedicated teachers, committed for the long term? Many argue that the greatest flaw of alternative certification programs generally, and of TFA in particular, is that they recruit talented people who are interested in teaching only for a few years in order to gain "life experience" or to bolster their résumé. After a brief stint in teaching, many of these people exit for graduate school or the corporate world. We can't build public school success, this argument goes, on a revolving-door teacher force.

Unsurprisingly, TFA teachers do leave the profession at higher rates than conventionally trained teachers. However, the differences in attrition rates are not nearly as drastic as we might anticipate. About a quarter of all teachers leave the profession in their first three years, and the attrition rates are much higher in the low-performing schools that employ TFA members.[13] According to a Harvard study, about 61 percent of TFA teachers who entered between 2002 and 2004 remained in the teaching profession longer than their two-year commitment. About 36 percent of TFA teachers remained employed as teachers for at least four years.[14] According to its own internal survey of program alumni, 63 percent of former TFA members throughout the program's twenty-year history remain professionally involved in public education to this day. About a third of the program's more than twenty thousand alumni continue to serve as public school teachers.[15]

But how concerning are higher attrition rates anyway?

We know that there is little relationship between teacher experience and effectiveness in the classroom. On average, teachers tend to improve during their first three to five years in the classroom. Thus most teachers who leave early in their careers do so before they have reached their full potential.

However, we also know that experience itself explains very little of the variation in teacher quality. Recall from our discussion in a previous chapter that experience, credentials, and other easily observable factors are responsible for around 3 to 5 percent of the difference in teachers. When we consider the effects of attrition on teacher quality, then, it is important that we focus on comparing one teacher to another, rather than comparing a particular teacher to his potential future self.

The research on TFA suggests that the higher attrition rates are not a real concern. The results of the Mathematica study, the only one to use a truly experimental approach, as well as several other quasi-experimental studies, suggest that new TFA teachers are at least as effective in the classroom as traditional teachers with six or more years of experience. If TFA teachers leave the classroom at high rates and are simply replaced by other alternatively certified teachers, the high attrition rate won't decrease teacher quality. A New York City study of alternatively certified teachers found that "even high turnover groups (such as Teach for America participants) would have to be only slightly more effective in their first year to offset the negative effects of their high exit rates."[16]

OPEN THE FLOODGATES

What all of this makes clear is that there is little need to require teachers to earn an education degree, at least as they are currently awarded. Teachers in training are not learning some magic skill during their college years that makes them better teachers. Nor is it particularly important that all teachers who enter the system demonstrate a commitment to spending twenty-five years in the classroom.

Not everyone, not even every Ivy League graduate, can teach. It takes a special person to be a great teacher. But what the positive experience of alternative certification programs shows is that education colleges are not providing future teachers with meaningful skills that cannot be acquired elsewhere. Nor does the training requirement only weed out individuals who would make poor teachers, a fact made clear by the enormous variation in the quality of conventionally trained teachers. The most important effect of the current system's training requirement is to deny many people with the potential to become great public school teachers their chance in the classroom.

Jane from our example might have been no better as a teacher than her roommate. But the only way to know that would have been to give her the opportunity and evaluate her performance.

A better policy would open the floodgates. Any college graduate who wants to give teaching a chance and can convince a principal to hire her should have the opportunity to teach. At the very least, we should allow for many pathways to teaching through multiple certification programs that are not affiliated with education colleges and do not require four years of training, and school systems should not discriminate against applicants because of their particular pathway.

Opening the classroom doors seems to be a scary thought. What assurances will there be that a new teacher who hasn't gone to an education college won't be a disaster in the classroom?

There are no such assurances. Many teachers who receive training outside of a college of education are bad teachers. There is wide variation in the quality of teachers who acquired an alternative certification from a program such as TFA. Some of the teachers are great, but some of these otherwise very talented individuals simply do not have what it takes to become effective teachers.

But the variation in effectiveness makes alternatively certified teachers no different from teachers who enter the classroom through the conventional routes. The current system provides a false sense of security. What we have learned over the past several years is that wide variation persists despite the training requirement.

Expanding the use of alternative certification—or rather, eliminating the requirement that teachers earn a degree from a college of education—could dramatically expand the pool of people who are willing to attempt teaching. That's a good thing.

But we should not expect to increase teacher quality dramatically simply by opening the door to a wider pool of applicants. Increasing the pool will increase quality only if we simultaneously institute policies that retain effective teachers while weeding out mediocre ones.

REMOVING INEFFECTIVE TEACHERS

We know that there are bad teachers in our public schools today. Principals, parents, and other teachers knew that was the case before empirical research showed that it was true. That basic fact raises an obvious question: why not simply remove those teachers we know are ineffective?

Clearly, students would be better off if ineffective teachers were taken out of the classroom. But as discussed previously, tenure is the most powerful force keeping bad teachers in our public schools.

Much like university professors, public school elementary and secondary teachers are eligible to receive tenure that provides them with powerful job protections. However, the process of earning tenure in public elementary and secondary schools is far less burdensome, and the rational basis for its existence far less compelling. Essentially, tenure ensures that experienced teachers cannot be fired without the benefit of a due-process proceeding. There once was a need for teaching-job protections, but that day has come and gone. Today's tenure system primarily serves to keep low-performing teachers in the classroom.

Tenure was instituted in public schools alongside the growth of teachers' unions in the mid-twentieth century. Tenure was a solution to real problems that had faced teachers since early days of public schooling. Administrators frequently mistreated teachers. There were many cases in which teachers were fired for holding the wrong political beliefs, for getting pregnant, or for speaking out against the operations of their schools. Elected officials could remove a teacher from a school in order to fill her position with a political patron or family member.[17]

In the early days, tenure very likely did protect teachers from wrongful termination. However, it has always also protected the jobs of teachers who are simply performing poorly. Even Albert Shanker, former head of the American Federation of Teachers and easily the most important figure in the early teacher unionization movement, recognized that tenure was protecting incompetent teachers.[18]

In the early days, considering the influence of tenure meant weighing the need to protect teachers from unjust action against the need to remove ineffective teachers. That isn't a very easy policy matter. Today, however, the scales have been tipped.

We do not want to go back to the days when administrators discriminated against teachers for their political beliefs or for starting families. Defenders of the tenure system argue that were it not for tenure, today's teachers would face the same discriminatory practices as in the 1930s. For instance, the only real defense for today's tenure system lodged by education historian Diane Ravitch in her book *The Death and Life of the Great American School System* is that

> [t]eachers have been fired for all sorts of dubious and non-meritorious reasons: for being of the wrong race or religion, for being gay or belonging to some other disfavored group, for not contributing to the right politician, for not paying a bribe to someone for their job, for speaking out on an issue outside the classroom, for disagreeing with the principal, or simply to make room for a school board member's sister, nephew, or brother-in-law.[19]

Protections against such actions might have been necessary in the early days of the labor movement in the United States, but they are at best redundant in modern labor law. There are a multitude of laws that protect workers from unfair discrimination by their employers. There is no real danger that removing tenure would bring back the days when women were fired for getting pregnant or when anyone was fired because of his race.

Of course, we do not live in a perfect world, and workplace discrimination does exist. But the legal system does more than an adequate job of protecting workers. Teachers were not the only employees treated poorly in the mid-twentieth century, and as a society we have gone a long way toward improving the lot of all workers. There is no reason to believe that teachers are more vulnerable to the malicious or capricious will of their employers than anyone else.

TENURE'S JOB PROTECTIONS

It is true, as its defenders like to argue, that tenure does not explicitly guarantee a public school teacher his job for life; it entitles him to a due-process proceeding before he is fired. On the surface, that seems to be a reasonable restriction: no one should be fired without an employer's providing a just cause. However, in practice the due process required to fire a tenured teacher is so burdensome and has such a low likelihood of success that most principals and school systems simply don't bother with it.

In virtually every state, the process for removing tenured teachers is overwhelmingly onerous. To fire a teacher for any reason—be it incompetence, malfeasance, or child abuse—can take several years, during which the teacher often remains in the classroom and is paid full salary and benefits. There are barriers at each point in the process, and even minor failures to comply with a time line or basic procedure is cause for dismissal of the case. The legal fees required to fire a single tenured teacher can reach into the hundreds of thousands of dollars.

Furthermore, even when school systems seek to take action against a very poor teacher, there is a high probability of failure. According to an analysis by the *Los Angeles Times*, even though the Los Angeles school district takes action against teachers in only the most serious cases, charged teachers win on appeal more than a third of the time.[20] Thus, while tenure does not explicitly guarantee a teacher's job, it serves as a strong enough protection to keep the vast majority of teachers in the classroom.

In New York City, for example, only forty-five tenured teachers were fired for any reason during the 2008 and 2009 school years combined.[21] On average, only about two tenured teachers in the entire state of Illinois are fired due to poor performance in the classroom each year.[22] During an eighteen-year period, 94 percent of districts in Illinois did not attempt to fire a single tenured teacher.[23] Between 1995 and 2005, the struggling Chicago public school system formally remediated a total of only 231 teachers,[24] a tiny fraction of its 27,039 public school teachers.[25] The situation is no better in California. Los Angeles fires an average of about one in one thousand teachers a year; Long Beach fires about six per one thousand teachers; San Diego, about two per one thousand teachers.[26]

Rarely is poor classroom performance cited as a reason for dismissal; it was not listed as a factor in 80 percent of the dismissals upheld in Los Angeles between 1994 and 2009.[27] Only eight of the terminations in New York City in 2008 and 2009 were related to the teacher's effectiveness, and six of those cases included other charges, such as insubordination or misconduct.[28]

Such powerful job protections have substantial negative consequences. Once granted tenure, teachers are essentially employed for life, even if they cannot teach at all.

Perhaps as importantly, by eliminating any chance of termination, tenure depresses motivation. Workers in the private sector know that they must meet some minimal standard for effectiveness if they are to keep their jobs. This basic incentive doesn't exist for public school teachers. To their great credit, the majority of teachers work very hard even knowing they can't be fired for slacking off. But there are still plenty of teachers who take advantage of their job protections.

GRANTING TEACHERS TENURE

All teachers—indeed, all employees in any sector—deserve basic protections from discrimination and irrational behavior from administrators. But protections powerful enough to make termination nearly impossible make no sense in any sector.

Unfortunately, school districts across the nation grant tenure without any serious consideration of the teacher's quality. Unlike at the university level, where tenure is a difficult process that takes place over several years, public school teachers are nearly uniformly granted tenure for little more than remaining in the classroom for a short period of time. The result is that there are many teachers in our public schools who don't deserve to be there.

Teachers become eligible for tenure very early in their careers. According to a 2008 evaluation of tenure laws by the National Council on Teacher Quality (NCTQ), in thirty-three states teachers become eligible for tenure after three years in the classroom, ten states make teachers eligible for tenure in fewer than three years, and in only two states—Indiana and Missouri—do teachers wait five years before they are eligible.[29]

In theory, teachers can be denied tenure and kept at the school on a probationary status. In practice, the vast majority of teachers who are eligible for tenure receive it. In New York City, for instance, only 234 of 6,386 teachers—about 3 percent—who were eligible to receive tenure in 2010 were denied. That actually represents a large increase in tenure denial, from a reform-minded public school system. In 2006, only twenty-five of the approximately 6,250 teachers eligible for tenure were denied. According to an analysis by the *Los Angeles Times*, less than 2 percent of eligible public school teachers in Los Angeles are denied tenure.[30]

None of this should be surprising when we recall that just about all teachers receive satisfactory performance evaluations. In theory, a teacher's performance in the classroom helps to determine whether she stays on the job. But without a real measure of the teacher's effectiveness, just about anyone who wants to remain in the classroom is allowed to do so.

When determining whether to grant teachers tenure, principals rarely consider any measure of the teacher's performance. In fact, according to the NCTQ review of tenure laws, only two states—Iowa and New Mexico—require that school systems evaluate a teacher's effectiveness before granting tenure.[31] In Los Angeles, teachers are often granted tenure after only a single preannounced classroom visit per year.[32]

Perhaps there is no better illustration of the laxity with which teachers are granted tenure than the process in New York City. The system's default procedure is to grant the teacher tenure unless the principal explicitly denies it and justifies her decision. That is, after only three years in the classroom, all teachers will be granted tenure unless a principal actively objects, which obviously happens only in the most extreme circumstances. A better system would flip that default—a teacher should be granted the privilege of tenure only if he demonstrates that he is an exceptional teacher.[33]

Some school systems are beginning to take seriously the need to consider a teacher's effectiveness before granting tenure. However, such efforts are being fought viciously in the political arena. New York, for instance, is in the process of developing an evaluation system that uses both quantitative and qualitative measures that will bear directly on tenure decisions. But this program was not put forward until a long and brutal political fight. In fact, teachers' unions had successfully lobbied the state legislature not to implement the new system before ultimately losing.[34]

REMOVING TEACHERS TAXPAYERS CAN'T AFFORD

Removing ineffective teachers is a no-brainer. But what about times when we need to remove teachers due to budget constraints?

For a variety of fiscal and political reasons, layoffs are rarer in the public sector than they are in the private sector. However, decades of overspending by states and the federal government (coupled with the untimely financial crisis surrounding the housing market) has forced upon this generation a new age of austerity. With public schools making up a big chunk of state and local expenditures, and teacher salaries and benefits accounting for the lion's share of those budgets, it is a clear and unfortunate fact that states and school districts must find ways to provide public education with fewer teachers than before. Mass teacher layoffs are currently under consideration throughout the nation, and they are likely to remain on the agenda for some time.

No one wants to lay off large numbers of teachers—students and teachers both suffer when we have to shrink the teaching force. But it is vitally important that any teacher layoffs are distributed in a manner that will do the least harm to students. If we adopt that reasonable goal, what we do currently is the worst possible alternative.

The current practice is this: when a school district lays off teachers due to financial cuts, those layoffs are primarily distributed according to seniority. Teachers are rank ordered according to the date on which they were officially hired, and the most recently hired teachers are cut until the required costs are saved. Schools are allowed to make exceptions for particular areas—for instance, they do not eliminate all of their science teachers or special-education teachers if they all happen to be the least senior in the system. But there is no discretion built in.

In the private sector, seniority-driven layoffs are relegated to heavily unionized occupations that involve mostly manual labor; they rarely appear in white-collar professions. A law firm that finds itself strapped for cash doesn't necessarily let go its most junior lawyers; it tends to lay off the least effective and the least profitable lawyers. When a private firm makes cuts to its advertising staff, it makes decisions about the revenues and costs the each employee represents. In fact, seniority can be a liability for employees facing layoffs in the private sector, because more senior employees often have bloated salaries that are not entirely justified by their contribution to the firm. Public schools are saddled with a system that, once again, protects teachers at the expense of students.

At this writing, fourteen states make it illegal for school systems to consider anything other than seniority when determining teacher layoffs. Since some of the nation's most populous states—California, New York, Illinois, Pennsylvania—are on that list, such laws currently apply to 39 percent of the nation's public school teachers. Thirty-two states do not specify in local law how layoffs are to be distributed, and in these cases collective bargaining agreements at the school-district level usually impose last-in-first-out requirements. Only three states—Colorado, Arizona, and Oklahoma—and the District of Columbia require that teacher performance play a major role in how layoffs are distributed.[35]

Layoff plans do not even incorporate the current flawed teacher evaluations. As discussed in chapter 2, it is common for 99 percent or more of teachers in public school districts to receive a positive rating. And yet when it comes to layoffs, even those few teachers identified as truly horrible are protected by seniority.

There must be a better way to lay off teachers when necessary. In fact, it is actually difficult to think of a system for determining teacher layoffs worse than one based on seniority.

Since seniority is not a reasonable proxy for teacher quality, basing firing decisions on experience makes no sense. Again, recall that while previous research shows that teachers improve during their first three to five years in the classroom, such experience explains very little of the difference between one teacher and another.

The result of seniority-based layoffs, then, is to reduce the number of teachers—and thus increase class size—but to have no effect on the distribution of teacher quality. Why? Because layoffs based on seniority are essentially no different from a random firing of teachers: some great young teachers will be let go, some terrible teachers will be let go, and a lot of teachers of about average quality will be let go. A layoff policy that drew the names of teachers out of a hat would have just about the same effect on teacher quality as a seniority-based layoff system.

Basing layoffs on seniority actually requires more teachers to be fired, because schools have to fire more (lower-paid) junior teachers in order to receive cost savings. This, of course, leads to larger class sizes as a result.

Theoretically, a plan that laid off the *most* senior teachers would be preferable. By removing the most expensive teachers, there would need to be fewer layoffs, with a less detrimental effect on class sizes.

Of course, the preferred system would target the least-effective teachers for layoffs.

Even many effective teachers are wary of tying layoffs to performance. That's in large part because in years past, that meant giving full discretion to principals and other administrators. As discussed, school administrators have not always been up to that task.

But no one who looked at the data or has spent any time in public schools honestly believes that laying off the youngest teachers is equivalent to laying off the least effective teachers: not parents, not teachers, not even union representatives. But from the teachers' perspective, the primary benefit of seniority-based layoff is that they are "fair," by which they mean nothing more than that they do not involve discretion that can be misapplied by vengeful or misguided administrators.

Fears are not unwarranted that administrators could abuse their power by targeting layoffs for their least-liked, rather than least-effective, teachers. However, we now have the tools necessary to evaluate teacher quality objectively. Thus we can target the least effective teachers for layoffs in a way that does not entirely depend on the discretion of principals. An evaluation system based on both quantitative and qualitative measures of a teacher's effectiveness—as we described in chapter 2—would be a fairly accurate way of determining which teachers are most expendable.

Researchers Donald Boyd, Hamilton Lankford, Susanna Loeb, and James Wyckoff recently used data from New York City to compare the effects of seniority-based layoffs to one targeting the worst teachers. Under a seniority-based plan, the city would need to reduce the number of fourth- and fifth-grade teachers by 7 percent, to reduce salaries by 5 percent. In order to reduce the cumulative salaries of fourth- and fifth-grade teachers by 5 percent, the city would need to let go 7 percent of its teachers under a seniority-based system. If the district instead removed teachers based on their estimated contribution to student learning, the city would have to reduce the teaching staff by only 5 percent, in order to save the same amount of money. But a targeted layoff would be more efficient, garnering a 5 percent cost reduction with just a 5 percent staff reduction. That is, a system that bases layoffs on a measure of effectiveness would lead to 25 percent fewer layoffs than a system based on seniority, and it would tend to keep higher-performing teachers in the classroom.[36]

Not surprisingly, the researchers found that only 13 percent of teachers who would be removed under a seniority-based system would also be removed under a system targeting the least-effective teachers.

Performance-based layoffs would *improve* the quality of public school teachers. If implemented with an eye toward teacher effectiveness, such layoffs would always tend to increase teacher quality by removing the lowest-performing teachers—this would be true even if there were only two teachers in the entire system, and you removed the less effective one.

Because of our failure to evaluate and fire poor-performing teachers, there are many we would be happy to remove from the classroom. Would targeted layoffs improve schools enough to outweigh the detrimental effects of increased class size? The vast variation in teacher quality suggests that would be the case. Removing bad teachers is that great a priority.

TRAINING vs. SELECTION

There are essentially two options available to improving teacher quality: either we dramatically revamp teacher education so that it offers a higher-quality product, or we find ways to improve the teacher workforce by altering the pool of those who choose to become teachers. The strategies are not mutually exclusive. But the promise offered by these strategies, and the time lines needed for each to produce substantial results, differ substantially.

There are several serious efforts underway to improve teacher education both within education colleges and from the outside. The Bill and Melinda Gates Foundation has funded an enormous effort to identify what makes an effective teacher and is developing training techniques that can be taught to new and experienced teachers alike. Teach for America recently published its own manual for training teachers.

While we should work to improve teacher training, we must be skeptical about the overall benefit. We haven't figured out how to train effective teachers so far—why do we think that we've finally solved that tricky puzzle?

Perhaps we will substantially improve teacher training in the next decade or so. Public schools will be much better off if we do. But efforts to improve the selection of teachers in public schools are more likely to produce results, are easier to implement, and can have a more immediate impact on public school quality than long-term efforts to improve colleges of education.

We now know that what makes one teacher better than another is often a series of characteristics that cannot be easily observed before the teacher enters the classroom. That's the consistent lesson of modern empirical research on teacher quality. The attributes that make one teacher more effective than another seem to be innate characteristics that are not learned in a college classroom. That's not to say that pedagogical skills are useless. But it appears that they can be discovered or instilled in a teacher on-the-job.

We should hire teachers with the assumption that they are capable of acquiring the skills necessary for success in the classroom. We should provide them with support during their early years in order to help them acquire those skills. And teachers who fail to acquire those skills should be removed from the classroom and replaced with promising new candidates.

8

CONCLUSION

Education-reform efforts are currently gaining broad political support. Policy makers, pundits, and intellectuals across the ideological spectrum are advocating many of the same policy changes I've recommended in this book, especially the need to identify teacher quality, reward effective teachers, and remove ineffective teachers. Even President Obama is a vocal supporter of performance pay and the removal of ineffective teachers. The very idea that a Democratic president would support these reforms was unthinkable less than a decade ago.

Emboldened school systems across the country are beginning to experiment with and enact many effective reforms. Pilot performance-pay programs now exist in several large school districts. Colorado and Florida have led the way toward eliminating lifetime tenure protections, and other states are considering similar proposals. Alternative certification programs have been growing rapidly. States across the nation are considering adopting more meaningful evaluation systems that use both qualitative and quantitative measures of a teacher's performance. The writing is on the wall: change is coming, sooner or later.

But we still need a clear picture of what effective reform looks like, and a comprehensive agenda for improving schools. To that end, I propose the following key points of any effective reform.

TOWARD A BETTER SYSTEM

The implications of modern research are harsh but clear: we fail to prevent potentially bad teachers from entering the classroom, and we fail to remove them before they become entrenched. Our inability to recognize effective teachers before they enter the classroom means that the screens imposed by the current system keep out as many great teachers as they do bad teachers. Since there is no actual link between a teacher's effectiveness and his education or background, we must instead evaluate teachers based on outputs—that is, their contribution to student learning. The vast differences in teacher quality mean that we can improve instruction in American classrooms by adopting policies that systematically remove ineffective teachers and retain the effective ones.

Meaningfully Evaluate Teacher Performance

The first and most important step is to identify systematically the best and worst teachers. No one honestly believes that all teachers are equally effective. The evaluation system should produce results reflecting that reality.

No other reform discussed in this book can work effectively without first adopting a tool capable of distinguishing between good teachers and poor ones. Evaluation is the bedrock on which all other reforms must be built.

Current evaluation systems are worse than useless, providing teachers with no feedback about their performance and providing principals with no useful information for differentiating employees. It promotes the lie that all teachers are essentially the same, when it is painfully obvious that some teachers are better than others.

A robust system will use both qualitative and quantitative tools to differentiate teachers. Only a decade ago, public schools did not have access to tools to develop real evaluation, but now they do. The explosion in standardized testing over the past decade and the resulting rich data sets storing that information now provide us with quantitative measures that can be combined with rigorous qualitative assessments. By combining both quantitative and qualitative measures, schools can develop meaningful and actionable information about a teacher's effectiveness that protects against the limitations of both tools. Quantitative measures of teacher quality are not influenced by personal biases and are not limited to considering observations of the human eye. Subjective evaluations by administrators can identify times when student test scores aren't telling the whole story about a teacher's contribution to the school or to her students' lives. Working together, qualitative and quantitative measures of teacher quality can provide a rich evaluation tool. There is no such thing as a perfect evaluation system in education or in any other profession. But it is clear that we have the tools necessary to improve dramatically upon the rubber-stamp evaluations used today.

Once we are able to distinguish between the best and worst teachers, the obvious next step is to use that information effectively. We know that there are great teachers and terrible teachers in our classrooms today. We should do something about it.

Remove Unnecessary Barriers to Becoming a Teacher

Since we cannot screen for effective teachers before they enter the classroom, I suggest that we open the floodgates. Any college graduate who can convince a principal to hire her should be given the opportunity to teach. Not everyone has what it takes to be a great teacher. But the ability to be a great teacher might be in anyone. Graduating with an education degree has no bearing on whether someone will be effective in the classroom, so lacking one should no longer shut out potentially great teachers.

Some of those who enter the classroom with little pedagogical training won't make it. Others will be fantastic educators. The expected variation in the quality of unconventionally trained teachers strikes some as a scary prospect. But in truth, it is no different from the status quo.

Removing the certification requirement will increase the number of potentially good teachers who make their way into the classroom. But since it will also open the door to many bad teachers, it's not a sufficient reform alone. We have to also change the way that we retain teachers.

Remove Ineffective Teachers

Everyone ostensibly agrees that bad teachers should be removed from the classroom. And yet, few schools make any serious effort to identify and remove them. No single education reform has more promise than liberating schools to remove lousy teachers from the classroom, once they have been identified.

Work rules that allow bad teachers to remain in the classroom for as long as they choose must be eliminated. When necessary, we also need to act swiftly to remove those who do not leave on their own. Certainly, teachers deserve to be protected from capricious or vindictive firings, but they require no more protections than other professionals. The job protections inherent to tenure are far too strong. Furthermore, no job protections should be granted without careful consideration of a teacher's worth in the classroom. Tenure should be treated as a privilege reserved for the best teachers who will serve as role models for others, not as a right to be granted to anyone who decides to stick around for a few years.

Pay Great Teachers More

We also need a system that rewards its best teachers with higher salaries. The current salary schedule is based on two factors—years of experience and credentials—which we know are unrelated to how well a teacher performs in the classroom. We give teachers generous incentives to earn degrees that are irrelevant to classroom performance. The result? Teachers earn advanced degrees and get paid more without regard to their actual performance!

A better compensation system would reward teachers who are making a difference in their students' lives. Differentiating the pay offered to higher- and lower-performing teachers would create an environment that is more likely to keep effective teachers than ineffective teachers. Great teachers are important, and they deserve to be rewarded for their contribution to society.

Good teachers should take home greater pay than they do today. Too much of a teacher's compensation is back-loaded in his retirement benefits. Teachers should own their own retirement plans, just like any other professional. A sensible retirement plan would take into account that some teachers aren't certain they want to spend their entire professional lives in the same job. It would also make it easier for burned-out teachers to leave the profession before they have overstayed their welcome. Moving more of a teacher's pay to her take-home salary would encourage young prospects to give teaching a try and would improve the quality of life associated with a teaching salary.

Overall, what would a new employment system for teachers look like? It is a system that imposes few barriers to entry and then differentiates between those teachers it wants to keep and those teachers it is happy to see try another profession. It is a system that recognizes great teachers with higher pay. It is a system that understands that not everyone who enters into a classroom is going to be a great teacher. It is a system that values great teachers and seeks to remove ineffective teachers. It is a system that benefits both teachers and students.

The proposals above reflect what we have learned over the past two decades from empirical research: teachers are important; teacher quality varies enormously; we must evaluate each teacher directly, and compensate teachers for outstanding results. Those basic and obvious facts are pushing us toward a system that distinguishes and values great teachers.

NOTES

INTRODUCTION

1. C. Goldin and L. F. Katz, *The Race between Education and Technology* (Cambridge, MA: Belknap Press, 2008).

2. See, for instance, Randi Weingarten, "Don't Scapegoat Teachers," *Washington Post*, October 17, 2010.

3. For a review of such research, see D. N. Figlio and H. F. Ladd, "School Accountability and Student Achievement," in *Handbook of Research in Education Finance and Policy*, ed. Helen F. Ladd and Edward B. Fisk (New York, NY: Routledge, 2008).

4. For a review or such research, see B. Gill and K. Booker, "School Competition and Student Outcomes," in Ladd and Fisk (2008).

5. Ibid.

CHAPTER 1

1. M. Lewis, *Moneyball: The Art of Winning an Unfair Game* (New York, NY: Norton, 2003).

2. See, for example, H. MacDonald, "New York's Indispensable Institution," *City Journal*, July 7, 2009.

3. See T. D. Cook, "Sciencephobia," *Education Next* (Fall 2001): 63–68; and J. D. Angirst, "American Education Research Changes Tack," *Oxford Review of Economic Policy* 20, no. 2 (2004): 1–15.

4. Cook, "Sciencephobia."

5. Ibid.

6. D. Koretz, *Measuring Up: What Educational Testing Really Tells Us* (Cambridge, MA: Harvard University Press, 2008).

7. E. Hanushek and F. Welsh, Preface to *Handbook of the Economics of Education*, vol. 1 (Amsterdam, NL: North-Holland, 2006).

8. US Department of Education, Institute for Education Sciences, National Center for Education Statistics, National Assessment of Educational Progress, 2009.

CHAPTER 2

1. Remarks by the president at "Open for Questions" town hall, March 26, 2009, http://www.whitehouse.gov/the_press_office/Remarks-by-the-President-at-Open-for-Questions-Town-Hall/ (accessed June 23, 2009).

2. J. Kozol, *Savage Inequalities: Children in America's Schools* (New York, NY: Harper Perennial, 1992), 46–52.

3. National Center for Education Statistics, Digest of Education Statistics 2010, table 68, http://nces.ed.gov/programs/digest/d10/ (accessed July 27, 2011).

4. Ibid., table 71.

5. US Department of Education, "New No Child Left Behind Flexibility: Highly Qualified Teachers," http://www.ed.gov/nclb/methods/teachers/hqtflexibility.html (accessed May 26, 2009).

6. E. Hanushek, "The Trade-off between Child Quantity and Quality," *The Journal of Political Economy* 100, no. 1 (1992): 84–117.

7. W. L. Sander and J. C. Rivers, "Cumulative and Residual Effects of Teachers on Future Student Academic Achievement," Research Progress Report, University of Tennessee Value-Added Research and Assessment Center, 1996.

8. J. E. Rockoff, "The Impact of Individual Teachers on Student Achievement: Evidence from Panel Data," *American Economic Review* 94, no. 2 (2004): 247–52.

9. D. Aaronson, L. Barrow, and W. Sander, "Teachers and Student Achievement in the Chicago Public High Schools," *Journal of Labor Economics* 25, no. 1 (2007): 95–135.

10. M. West and M. Chingos, "Teacher Effectiveness, Mobility, and Attrition in Florida: A Descriptive Analysis," paper prepared for the Performance Incentives: Their Growing Impact on American K–12 Education conference hosted by The National Center on Performance Incentives, February 28–29, 2008.

11. S. G. Rivkin, E. A. Hanushek, and J. F. Kain, "Teachers, Schools, and Academic Achievement," *Econometrica* 73, no. 2 (2005): 417–58.

12. For instance, see Special Issue: Key Issues in Value-Added Modeling, *Education Finance and Policy* 3, no. 4 (Fall 2009).

13. American Federation of Teachers, "Hot Topics: Teacher Quality," http://www.aft.org/topics/teacher-quality/index.htm (accessed November 17, 2009).

14. E. A. Hanushek and S. G. Rivkin, "Teacher Quality," in *Handbook of The Economics of Education,* vol. 1, ed. Eric Hanushek and Finis Welsh (Amsterdam, NL: North-Holland, 2006).

15. See T. J. Kane, J. E. Rockoff, and D. O. Staiger, "What Does Certification Tell Us About Teacher Effectiveness? Evidence from New York City," *Economics of Education Review* 27, no. 6 (2008): 615–31. A possible exception is whether or not a teacher is National Board Certified; see D. Goldhaber and Anthony, "Can Teacher Quality Be Effectively Assessed? National Board Certification as a Signal of Effective Teaching," *The Review of Economics and Statistics* 89, no. 1 (2007): 134–50; S. Cantrell, J. Fullerton, T. J. Kane, D. O. Staiger, "National Board Certification and Teacher Effectiveness: Evidence from a Random Assignment Experiment," NBER Working Paper No. 14608, 2008. However, it is unclear from this work whether National Board Certified teachers are more effective because of their additional training or because highly effective teachers are more likely to attempt to gain this certification.

16. D. N. Harris and T. R. Sass, "Teacher Training, Teacher Quality, and Student Achievement," unpublished manuscript, 2008.

17. Ibid.

18. D. Goldhaber, "The Mystery of Good Teaching," *Education Next* 2, no. 1 (Spring 2002): 50–55.

19. Jonah E. Rockoff, Brian A. Jacob, Thomas J. Kane, and Douglas O. Staiger, "Can You Recognize an Effective Teacher When You Recruit One?," *Education Finance and Policy* 6, no. 1 (2011): 43–74.

CHAPTER 3

1. Remarks by the secretary in his address to the Fourth Annual Institute for Education Sciences Research Conference, June 8, 2009, http://www.ed.gov /news/speeches/2009/06/06082009.html (accessed July 22, 2009).

2. D. Weisberg, S. Sexton, J. Mulhern, and D. Keeling, "The Widget Effect: Our National Failure to Acknowledge and Act on Differences in Teacher Effectiveness," New Teacher Project, 2009.

3. The NAEP Reading Achievement Levels by Grade, http://nces.ed.gov /nationsreportcard/Reading/achieveall.asp (accessed July 22, 2009).

4. P. Cramer, "Number of Teachers Rated Unsatisfactory Rose Again Last Year," *Gotham Schools,* July 29, 2010, http://gothamschools.org/2010/07/29/number-of-teachers-rated-unsatisfactory-rose-again-last-year/ (accessed July 27, 2011).

5. Weisberg et al., "The Widget Effect."

6. The New Teacher Project, "Hiring, Assignment, and Transfer in Chicago Public Schools," 2007, http://tntp.org/files/TNTPAnalysis-Chicago.pdf (accessed July 27, 2011).

7. Margaret Downing, "In HISD There Are No Unsatisfactory Teachers: Surprise: We Live in Lake Woebegone," *Houston Press Blog*, April 29, 2010, http://blogs.houstonpress.com/hairballs/2010/04/in_hisd_there_are_no_unsatisfa.php (accessed December 17, 2010).

8. Edward C. Elliott, "City School Supervision: A Constructive Study Applied to New York City," part of the School Efficiency Series, ed. Paul H. Hanus (Chicago, IL: World Book Company, 1914).

9. S. Farr, *Teaching as Leadership: The Highly Effective Teacher's Guide to Closing the Achievement Gap* (Hoboken, NJ: Jossey-Bass, 2010).

10. E. Green, "Building a Better Teacher," *New York Times Magazine*, March 2, 2010.

11. L. Goe, C. Bell, and O. Little, "Approaches to Evaluating Teacher Effectiveness: A Research Synthesis," National Comprehensive Center for Teacher Quality, 2008.

12. C. Brandt, C. Mathers, M. Olivia, M. Brown-Sims, and J. Hess, "Examining District Guidance to Schools on Teacher Evaluation Policies in the Midwest Region," Institute of Education Sciences, US Department of Education, 2007.

13. The New Teacher Project, "Hiring, Assignment, and Transfer in Chicago Public Schools."

14. Los Angeles Unified teacher contract, Article X, 3.0.

15. Miami-Dade Unified teacher contract, Article XIII, Section 4, B.

16. B. A. Jacob and L. Lefgren, "Principals as Agents: Subjective Performance Measurement in Education," National Bureau of Economic Research, Working Paper No. 11463, 2005.

17. The New Teacher Project, "Hiring, Assignment, and Transfer in Chicago Public Schools."

18. "The MetLife Survey of the American Teacher: Transitions and the Role of Supportive Relationships 2004–2005," MetLife Foundation, June 14, 2005.

19. Los Angeles Unified teacher contract, Article X, Section 6.3.

20. The New Teacher Project, "Hiring, Assignment, and Transfer in Chicago Public Schools."

21. Ibid.

22. Ibid.

23. M. E. Lucas and D. Figlio, "The Gentleman's A," *Education Next* 4, no. 2 (Spring 2004): 60–68.

24. Dan Goldhaber and Michael Hansen, "Using Performance on the Job to Inform Teacher Tenure Decisions," *American Economic Review: Papers & Proceedings* 100 (2010): 250–55.

25. Steven Glazerman, Susanna Loeb, Dan Goldhaber, Douglas Staiger, Stephen Raudenbush, and Grover Whitehurst, "Evaluating Teachers: The Important Role of Value-Added," Brookings Institution, November 17, 2010, http://www.brookings.edu/reports/2010/1117_evaluating_teachers.aspx (accessed July 27, 2011).

26. Goldhaber and Hansen, "Using Performance on the Job to Inform Teacher Tenure Decisions."

27. D. N. Figlio, and H. F. Ladd, "School Competition and Student Outcomes," in *Handbook of Research in Education Finance and Policy*, ed. Helen F. Ladd and Edward B. Fiske (New York, NY: Routledge, 2007).

28. B. A. Jacob and L. Lefgren, "Principals as Agents: Subjective Performance Measurement in Education," NBER Working Paper No. 11463, 2005.

29. Data Quality Campaign, 2008 Survey Results, http://www.dataqualitycampaign.org/survey (accessed July 31, 2009).

CHAPTER 4

1. W. Elsbree, *The American Teacher: Evolution of a Profession in a Democracy* (New York, NY: American Book Company, 1887), 439–40.

2. Charles Bartlett Dyke, "Economic Aspect of Teachers' Salaries," *Columbia University Contributions to Philosophy, Psychology and Education* 7, no. 2 (New York, NY: Macmillan, 1899).

3. Dyke cites "the latest report of the Commissioner of Education (1896–97)" in "Economic Aspect of Teachers' Salaries," 47.

4. Ibid., 47–48.

5. As reported in Dyke's "Economic Aspect of Teachers' Salaries," 45.

6. For example, see D. Ravitch, *The Great School Wars: A History of the New York City Public Schools* (Baltimore, MD: The Johns Hopkins University Press, 1974).

7. R. J. Murnane and David K. Cohen, "Merit Pay and the Evaluation Problem: Understanding Why Most Merit Pay Plans Fail and Few Survive," *Harvard Educational Review* 56, no. 1 (1986): 1–18.

8. Elsbree, *The American Teacher*.

9. E. S. Evenden, "Teachers' Salaries and Salary Schedules in the United States, 1918–1919," prepared for the Commission on the Emergency in Education of the National Education Association, 1919, 119–20.

10. Ibid., 119.

11. Paul J. Porwoll, *Merit Pay for Teachers* (Arlington, VA: Educational Research Service, 1979).

12. National Center for Education Statistics, Digest of Education Statistics 2009, table 75, http://nces.ed.gov/programs/digest/d09/ (accessed July 27, 2011).

13. Bureau of Labor Statistics, May 2009 National Occupational Employment and Wage Estimates, United States, http://www.bls.gov/oes/current/oes_nat .htm (accessed December 21, 2010).

14. National Center for Education Statistics, Digest of Education Statistics 2009, table 75.

15. Frederick M. Hess, "Teacher Quality, Teacher Pay," American Enterprise Institute Policy Review, April/May 2004, http://www.frederickhess.org/5054 /teacher-quality-teacher-pay (accessed December 21, 2010).

16. Bureau of Labor Statistics, May 2009 National Occupational Employment and Wage Estimates, United States.

17. National Center for Education Statistics, Digest of Education Statistics 2009, table 78.

18. E. Hanushek and S. Rivkin, "Teacher Quality," in *Handbook of the Economics of Education*, vol. 2, ed. E. Hanushek and F. Welch (Amsterdam, NL: North-Holland, 2006), 1054.

19. Bureau of Labor Statistics, May 2009 National Occupational Employment and Wage Estimates, United States.

20. National Center for Education Statistics, Digest of Education Statistics 2009, table 69.

21. Ibid.

22. Average salaries come from the Occupational Employment Statistics and Wage Survey made publicly available by the New Jersey Department of Labor and Workforce Development.

23. The number of required hours worked varies by school system. For this calculation we use the required number of hours worked in Newark, which is the state's largest public school district.

CHAPTER 5

1. M. A. Spence, "Job Market Signaling," *Quarterly Journal of Economics* 87, no. 3 (1973): 355–74.

2. National Center for Education Statistics, Digest of Education Statistics 2009, tables 76 and 77, http://nces.ed.gov/programs/digest/d09/ (accessed July 27, 2011).

3. National Center for Education Statistics, Digest of Education Statistics 2010, table 73, http://nces.ed.gov/programs/digest/d10/ (accessed July 27, 2011).

4. E. Hanushek and S. Rivkin, "Teacher Quality," in *Handbook of the Economics of Education*, vol. 2, ed. E. Hanushek and F. Welch (Amsterdam, NL: North-Holland, 2006).

5. S. Corcoran, W. Evans, and R. Schwab, "Changing Labor-Market Opportunities for Women and the Quality of Teachers, 1957–2000," *American Economic Review* 94, no. 2 (2004): 230–35; M. P. Bacolod, "Do Alternative Opportunities Matter? The Role of Female Labor Markets in the Decline of Teacher Quality," *Review of Economics and Statistics* 89, no. 4 (2007): 737–51.

6. Corcoran, Evans, and Schwab, "Changing Labor-Market Opportunities for Women and the Quality of Teachers, 1957–2000"; Bacolod, "Do Alternative Opportunities Matter?"; C. M. Hoxby and A. Leigh, "Pulled Away or Pushed Out? Explaining the Decline in Teacher Aptitude in the United States," *AEA Papers and Proceedings* 49, no. 2 (2004): 236–40.

7. National Center for Education Statistics, Digest of Education Statistics 2009, table 78.

8. A. D. Roy, "Some Thoughts on the Distribution of Earnings," *Oxford Economic Papers* 3, no. 2 (1951): 135–46.

9. Hoxby and Leigh, "Pulled Away or Pushed Out?"

10. D. Goldhaber, B. Gross, and D. Player, *Are Public Schools Really Losing Their Best? Assessing the Career Transitions of Teachers and Their Implications for the Quality of the Teacher Workforce* (Washington, DC: National Center for Analysis of Longitudinal Data in Education Research, 2007).

11. D. Goldhaber, M. DeArmond, A. Liu, and D. Player, *Returns to Skill and Teacher Wage Premiums: What Can We Learn by Comparing the Teacher and Private Sector Labor Markets?* (Seattle: Center on Reinventing Public Education, 2008).

12. R. J. Murnane and D. Cohen, "Merit Pay and the Evaluation Problem: Why Most Merit Pay Plans Fail and Few Survive," *Harvard Education Review* 56, no. 1 (1986): 1–18.

13. K. Muralidharan and V. Sundararaman, "Teacher Incentives in Developing Countries: Experimental Evidence from India," Working Paper, National Center on Performance Incentives, Nashville, TN, 2008.

14. P. Glewwe, N. Ilias, and M. Kremer, "Teacher Incentives," Working Paper 9671, National Bureau for Economic Research, Cambridge, MA, 2003.

15. V. Lavy, "Evaluating the Effect of Teachers' Group Performance Incentives on Pupil Achievement," *Journal of Political Economy* 110, no. 6 (2002): 1286–1317.

16. M. G. Springer, D. Ballou, L. Hamilton, V. Le, J. R. Lockwood, D. F. MaCaffrey, M. Pepper, and B. M. Stecher, "Teacher Pay for Performance: Experimental Evidence from the Project on Incentives in Teaching," National Center on Performance Incentives, Nashville, TN, 2010.

17. M. Springer and M. A. Winters, "The NYC Teacher Pay for Performance Program: Early Evidence from a Randomized Field Trial," Manhattan Institute, *Civic Report* 56, April 2009.

18. D. N. Figlio and L. W. Kenny, "Individual Teacher Incentives and Student Performance," *Journal of Public Economics* 91 (2007): 901–14.

19. S. Hudson, "The Effects of Performance-Based Teacher Pay on Student Achievement," Stanford Institute for Economic Policy Research, Stanford, CA, 2010.

20. J. Coggshall, G. E. Behrstock-Sherrat, and K. Drill, "Workplaces that Support High-Performing Teaching and Learning: Insights from Generation Y Teachers," American Federation of Teachers, 2011.

CHAPTER 6

1. Robert M. Costrell and Michael Podgursky, "Peaks, Cliffs, and Valleys," *Education Next* 8, no. 1 (2008): 22–28.

2. Janet S. Hansen, "An Introduction to Teacher Retirement Benefits," *Education Finance and Policy* 5, no. 4 (2010): 402–37.

3. Katherine Barrett and Richard Greene, "Promises with a Price: Public Sector Retirement Benefits," PEW Center on the States, 2008, http://sao.hr.state.tx.us/features/pension_report.pdf (accessed July 27, 2011).

4. Frederick M. Hess and Juliet P. Squire, "'But the Pension Fund Was Just *Sitting* There . . .': The Politics of Teacher Retirement Plans," *Education Finance and Policy* 5, no. 4 (2010): 587–616.

5. Robert M. Costrell and Michael Podgursky, "Distribution of Benefits in Teacher Retirement Systems and their Implications for Mobility," *Education Finance and Policy* 5, no. 4 (2004): 519–57.

6. Michael DeArmond and Dan Goldhaber, "Scrambling the Next Egg: How Well Do Teachers Understand Their Pensions, and What Do They Think about Alternative Pension Structures?," *Education Finance and Policy* 5, no. 4 (2010): 558–86.

7. Robert M. Costrell, "Oh, To Be a Teacher in Wisconsin," *Wall Street Journal*, February 25, 2011.

8. Joel Klein, "Why Teacher Pensions Don't Work," *Wall Street Journal*, January 10, 2011.

9. Ibid.

10. Costrell and Podgursky, "Distribution of Benefits in Teacher Retirement Systems and their Implications for Mobility."

CHAPTER 7

1. David F. Labaree, "An Uneasy Relationship: The History of Teacher Education in the University," in *Handbook of Research on Teacher Education*, 3rd ed.,

ed. Marilyn Cochran-Smith, Sharon Feiman-Nemser, D. John McIntyre, and Kelly E. Demers (New York, NY: Routledge, 2008).

2. Ibid.

3. Arthur Levine, *Educating School Teachers* (Washington, DC: The Education Schools Project, 2006).

4. Ibid., 23.

5. Andrew J. Rotherham, "Teach for America: 5 Myths that Persist 20 Years On," *Time*, February 10, 2011.

6. Teach for America, "Our Impact," http://www.teachforamerica.org /what-we-do/our-impact/ (accessed February 25, 2011).

7. Teach for America, "Our Corps Members," http://www.teachforamerica .org/the-corps-experience/our-corps-members/ (accessed February 25, 2011).

8. Wendy Kopp's acceptance at the Manhattan Institute's Hamilton Awards Dinner, April 28, 2010.

9. Paul T. Decker, Daniel P. Mayer, and Steven Glazerman, *The Effects of Teach for America on Students: Findings from a National Evaluation* (Princeton, NJ: Mathematica Policy Research, Inc., 2004).

10. See, for instance, T. J. Kane, J. E. Rokoff, and D. O. Staiger, "What Does Certification Tell Us about Teacher Effectiveness? Evidence from New York City," NBER Working Paper 12155, 2006; M. Raymond, S. Fletcher, and J. Luque, "Teach for America: An Evaluation of Teacher Differences and Student Outcomes in Houston Texas," Center for Research on Education Outcomes, 2001; Z. Xu, J. Hannaway, and C. Taylor, "Making a Difference? The Effects of Teach for America in High School," Urban Institute, 2007; D. Boyd, P. Grossman, K. Hammerness, H. Lankford, S. Loeb, M. Ronfeldt, and J. Wyckoff, "Recruiting Effective Math Teachers: How Do Math Immersion Teachers Compare? Evidence from New York City," unpublished manuscript, 2009.

11. See, for instance, D. Boyd, P. Grossman, H. Lankford, S. Loeb, and J. Wyckoff, "How Changes in Entry Requirements Alter the Teacher Workforce and Affect Student Achievement," *Education Finance and Policy* 1, no. 2 (2006): 176–216; L. Darling-Hammond, D. Holtzman, S. J. Gatlin, and J. V. Heillig, "Does Teacher Preparation Matter? Evidence about Teacher Certification, Teach for America, and Teacher Effectiveness," *Education Policy Analysis Archives* 13, no. 42 (2005): 1–48.

12. Wendy Kopp on Charlie Rose, July 1, 2008; *Teacher Attrition and Mobility: Results from the 2004–05 Teacher Follow-up Survey* (Washington, DC: US Department of Education, 2007).

13. *Teacher Attrition and Mobility: Results from the 2004–05 Teacher Follow-up Survey.*

14. Morgaen L. Donaldson, "Teach for America Teachers' Careers: Whether, When, and Why They Leave Low-Income Schools and the Teaching Profession," Harvard Graduate School of Education, 2008.

15. Teach for America, Alumni Social Impact Report—2009, http://www.teachforamerica.org/mission/documents/2009_ASIR_Final.pdf (accessed February 26, 2011).

16. Thomas J. Kane, Jonah E. Rockoff, and Douglas O. Staiger, "What Does Certification Tell Us About Teacher Effectiveness? Evidence from New York City," NBER Working Paper No. 12155, 2006.

17. See, for instance, D. Ravitch, *The Great School Wars: A History of the New York City Public Schools* (Baltimore, MD: Johns Hopkins University Press, 1974); Richard D. Kahlenberg, *Tough Liberal: Albert Shanker and the Battles over Schools, Unions, Race, and Democracy* (New York, NY: Columbia University Press, 2007).

18. Kahlenberg, *Tough Liberal*.

19. D. Ravitch, *The Death and Life of the Great American School System: How Testing and Choice are Undermining Education* (New York, NY: Basic Books, 2010), 176.

20. Jason Song, "Firing Teachers Can Be a Costly and Tortuous Task," *Los Angeles Times*, May 3, 2009.

21. Author's e-mail correspondence with US Department of Education.

22. S. Reader, "The Hidden Costs of Tenure," http://thehiddencostsoftenure.com/(accessed April 12, 2011).

23. Ibid.

24. "Formal Remediations Undertaken by Illinois Schools 1995–2005," The Hidden Costs of Tenure, http://thehiddencostsoftenure.com/district_remediations.html (accessed February 28, 2011).

25. National Center for Education Statistics, Digest of Education Statistics 2007, table 87, http://nces.ed.gov/pubs2008/2008022.pdf (accessed July 27, 2011).

26. Song, "Firing Teachers Can Be a Costly and Tortuous Task."

27. Ibid.

28. Author's e-mail correspondence with US Department of Education.

29. National Council on Teacher Quality, *State Teacher Policy Yearbook: What States Can Do to Retain Effective New Teachers*, 2008, http://www.nctq.org/stpy08/reports/stpy_national.pdf (accessed July 27, 2011).

30. Jason Felch, Jessica Garrison, and Jason Song, "Bar Set Low for Lifetime Job in L.A. Schools," *Los Angeles Times*, December 20, 2009.

31. National Council on Teacher Quality, *State Teacher Policy Yearbook: What States Can Do To Retain Effective New Teachers*, 2008.

32. Felch, Garrison, and Song, "Bar Set Low for Lifetime Job in L.A. Schools."

33. Anna Phillips, "City Unveils New Steps Designed to Make Path to Tenure Tougher," *Gotham Schools*, December 13, 2010.

34. Ibid.

35. New Teacher Project, "The Case Against Quality-blind Teacher Layoffs," 2011, http://tntp.org/publications/issue-analysis/the-case-against-quality-blind-layoffs/ (accessed July 27, 2011).

36. Donald J. Boyd, Hamilton Lankford, Susanna Loeb, and James H. Wyckoff, "Teacher Layoffs: An Empirical Illustration of Seniority vs. Measures of Effectiveness," Urban Institute, 2010, http://www.urban.org/uploadedpdf/1001421-teacher-layoffs.pdf (accessed July 27, 2011).

INDEX

ABOUT THE AUTHOR

Marcus A. Winters is senior fellow at the Manhattan Institute. His research has appeared in several academic journals including *Education Finance and Policy*, *Economics of Education Review*, and *Teachers College Record*. In addition, his articles and op-eds have appeared in *The Wall Street Journal*, *New York Daily News*, *LA Times*, *New York Post*, *City Journal*, and *National Review*.